The Mistresses of
George I and II

Dedication

To the Rakish Colonial and our two wonderful girls, for everything.

The Mistresses of George I and II

A Maypole and a Peevish Beast

Catherine Curzon

PEN & SWORD
HISTORY

First published in Great Britain in 2021 by
Pen & Sword History
An imprint of
Pen & Sword Books Ltd
Yorkshire – Philadelphia

ISBN 978 1 52676 272 6

A CIP catalogue record for this book is
available from the British Library.

Typeset by Mac Style
Printed and bound by CPI Group (UK) Ltd,
Croydon, CR0 4YY

Pen & Sword Books Limited incorporates the imprints of Atlas,
Archaeology, Aviation, Discovery, Family History, Fiction, History,
Maritime, Military, Military Classics, Politics, Select, Transport,
True Crime, Air World, Frontline Publishing, Leo Cooper, Remember
When, Seaforth Publishing, The Praetorian Press, Wharncliffe
Local History, Wharncliffe Transport, Wharncliffe True Crime
and White Owl.

For a complete list of Pen & Sword titles please contact

PEN & SWORD BOOKS LIMITED
47 Church Street, Barnsley, South Yorkshire, S70 2AS, England
E-mail: enquiries@pen-and-sword.co.uk
Website: www.pen-and-sword.co.uk

Or

PEN AND SWORD BOOKS
1950 Lawrence Rd, Havertown, PA 19083, USA
E-mail: Uspen-and-sword@casematepublishers.com
Website: www.penandswordbooks.com

Contents

Illustrations

Acknowledgements

As ever, huge thanks to the team at Pen & Sword, especially Jon and Laura for steering me right, not to mention my fierce and fabulous editor, Lucy!

It never fails to make me thoroughly chuffed that people can't get enough of the glorious Georgians, so to all of those who live for the long eighteenth century, I salute you. Glasses are raised to Adrian, Rob, Kathy, and Debra, because what's more fitting than gin to celebrate a couple of mistresses?

Last but in no universe least, massive hugs are thrown with abandon at Pippa, Nelly, and the Rakish Colonial – you rock!

Introduction

"We are ruined by trulls. Nay, what is more vexatious, by old ugly trulls, such as could not find entertainment in the most hospitable hundreds of Old Drury."[1]

Over the centuries, for better or worse, countless monarchs have ruled countless kingdoms. Some of them have been forgotten, some of them have been celebrated. Some were benevolent, some tyrannical, but there was one thing they could agree on: marriage was a serious business. And *business* was the operative word. When a monarch or their heir took a spouse, the decision was often one of politics rather than romance. The wrong choice of a significant other might have ramifications that could shatter a kingdom, whilst the right ring on the right finger had the power to expand an empire, stuff even the most ailing coffers full of gold or cement a conquering dynasty for centuries.

That's not to say that royal matches haven't been made for love, nor that those made for duty couldn't turn into devoted partnerships, but for every love match, there were plenty that began and ended as business. Some of these were famously disastrous, some made it work against the odds, and some hovered in between thanks to tolerance, patience or even the odd bit of extramarital dabbling. Yet whether famous or forgotten, all of these marriages had one duty at their heart: to secure succession.

The line of royal succession is the key to immortality. Play the game right and your line could rule for centuries. Get it wrong and it might be cut off, reducing a sovereign to a withered branch on the family tree. To secure the heir and the spare, or even better, *spares*, was the duty of every royal couple. A royal marriage was a job for life.

There was one thing that royal wives had to tolerate that their husbands didn't. The mistress, or *maîtresse-en-titre*, as she was known in France, was

---

1. *Mist's Journal.* 27 May 1721.

as much a part of the court as the monarch's ministers, regarded by some as a political marvel, by others as an avaricious tart. Yet if the modern understanding of a royal mistress is a woman whose role was purely decorative or sexual, that was far from the case in Georgian times. In fact, it was a hard-won position and one that some ladies had to employ all their wiles to cling onto. As you'll see, in the case of one of the two subjects of this book, the king's mistress was a lot more desperate to let go than to hang on.

Melusine von der Schulenberg and Henrietta Howard were two of the Georgian era's most enduring royal mistresses. At the courts of George I and George II respectively, one became a surrogate wife, the other a necessary evil. Their journeys to the king's bed were different but both joined households that were riven with misery and competition, where ambition ran rampant and gossip fuelled the flames. For Melusine, that journey included divorce, murder, and the near ruin of a country, whilst in the case of Henrietta, sanctuary from her brutal husband came at the cost of her only child's love. Melusine had no queen to contend with, but Henrietta was the servant to her lover's formidable bride, Caroline of Ansbach. It was a fundamental difference. George I made his mistress his one and only – most of the time – whilst for George II, the number one mistress would always be second best.

With palace apartments and the ear of the monarch supposedly theirs to command, both women enjoyed a rank and prestige that seemed to suggest their lives might be fairy tales. In fact, they were far from it. These are the stories of Melusine, Duchess of Kendal, and Henrietta, Countess of Suffolk, the principal mistresses at the fractured, feuding courts of King George I and his son, King George II. This is also the story of a changing world, as Stuart gave way to Hanoverian and the family from Germany began their reign on the throne of Great Britain.

Act I

Ehrengard Melusine von der Schulenberg, Duchess of Kendal

(25 December 1667–10 May 1743)

The Girl from Emden

On Christmas Day 1667, in the town of Emden, Brandenburg, Ehrengard Melusine von der Schulenberg was born. Why her parents, Gustavus Adolphus, Baron von der Schulenberg, and his wife, Petronella Ottilia von Schwencken, chose *Melusine* as a middle name is lost to the mists of time, but it was the name by which she was always known. The other Melusine was a figure of ancient mythology, a freshwater mermaid of fairy blood who ensnared monarchs and heroes throughout history and whose story was told in innumerable legends from folklore across the continent. Perhaps the future for the little girl born in Emden was written in her name.

Melusine von der Schulenberg, of course, was no creature of myth and legend, nor did she exist only in the pages of folklore. Instead she was a flesh and blood woman, a minor noble who, through her intimate relationship with King George I, rose higher than she might ever have dreamed. She left behind the genteel, ennobled poverty of her roots to forge a life of notoriety as the woman who sat as close to one of the most powerful thrones in the world as any uncrowned, unmarried mistress could hope to get. Melusine was set to become a queen in all but name.

There was little that was remarkable about the young Melusine's formative years, certainly nothing that would mark her out as a social climber to be watched as she navigated the road to St James's Palace. In fact, this apparent lack of ambition, coupled with an ability to know just what was required of her and when, was precisely what later endeared Melusine to the taciturn, sullen George Louis in Hanover. As we shall learn, the first Georgian king didn't look for a challenging partner, nor one who would be minded to argue with him, or even worse, a woman who might be driven to strike out on her own. George Louis' upbringing had forged a phlegmatic, emotionally withdrawn man whose outbursts of temper were rare but violent. His dedication to improving his family name and territorial fortunes was matched only by his ambition, which he had inherited from his ruthless father. When George Louis' wife, Sophia Dorothea, proved to be as emotional as he was repressed, it set the stage for disaster. Melusine, as we will see, was far better suited to George Louis than his wife would ever be.

But all of that is for later.

Melusine's mother, Petronella Ottilia, could trace her noble Westphalian line back through the generations to the thirteenth century, so whilst the family may not have had much money to burn nor the finest estates to call their own, they had something that was valued even more highly within their circle: good breeding. The blood of a respected noble line could plug the gaps left by a lack of ready cash and with his marriage to Petronella Ottilia, Gustavus Adolphus was able to bask in her reflected familial glory. But Gustavus Adolphus was no slouch himself. With his heart set on a political career he joined the household of the Elector of Brandenburg, where he soon acquired a reputation as a man who could get things done. Eventually Gustavus Adolphus would rise to the esteemed rank of privy councillor, but his stellar career meant that he was rarely at the family home in Emden. Instead the management of the household was left in the more than capable hands of Petronella Ottilia.

Gustavus Adolphus and Petronella Ottilia had nine children, three of whom died in infancy. Melusine was their fourth child and second daughter, and just like noble young ladies before her had been for generations, she was to be trained in all the skills necessary to make her way in the world. The seventeenth century was not a time when women were expected to forge ahead alone. Instead their prospects – especially if they were of noble stock like Melusine – came from their value as a bride. With her excellent heritage and her father's secure and respected position in Brandenburg, Melusine's value could not be underestimated. She spent her childhood being educated in the necessary feminine arts that would stand her in good stead for the throne room and the drawing room alike, preparing for the life that would one day await her. Melusine was in training to become a wife.

Though Petronella Ottilia oversaw her daughter's early education, Melusine had only a few scant years to spend with her mother. Petronella Ottilia died just a week after she delivered her last child in 1674, leaving her children motherless. Melusine was only six, and the death of her mother created a yawning chasm at the heart of the castle in Emden.

Melusine's early life really couldn't have been any more different from that of the woman who would later become her perceived rival, Sophia Dorothea of Celle. Sophia Dorothea was George I's cousin and eventually his wife, though they hated each other with a white-hot passion. Whilst Melusine had grown up motherless in a far from fairy tale castle among siblings who clung together after the loss of their mother, Sophia Dorothea had everything that Melusine did not. She was an only child, raised as a princess in a glittering castle that sat at the heart of a duchy that overflowed with wealth. Sophia Dorothea was the centre of attention and loved to be paraded through the streets in ribbons and silks by her adoring mother, where she was showered with gifts and shown off to the crowds who gathered to catch a glimpse of the pretty princess. Years later though, George Louis' sour-faced dislike of too much show and flightiness would be one of the things that drew him to Melusine, even as he kept his wife at arm's length. And when even that wasn't far enough, locking her away and trying to forget about her became his preferred solution.

With the untimely death of Petronella Ottilia, the foundations were laid for one of the tightest-knit families that could be found amongst the inner circle of Hanoverian royalty. Years later, when Melusine bore George Louis three children, her siblings would raise them as their own without balking. These weren't brothers and sisters riven with rivalry and clawing to outdo one another, but a little group that forged itself from grief. It was a support system that the House of Hanover would never be able to match as long as George I and George II sat at its head.

Over the years that have passed since Melusine's death, many have concluded that her primary motivation was financial. She was depicted as a venal, conniving shrew who had set out to capture a man with money and power – and succeeded. Of course, this is more than a little simplistic, but there were many reasons to become a mistress. In some cases, it was a desire for influence or cash whilst in others, it was a question of genuine affection, and though Melusine certainly enjoyed money, there was more to her relationship with King George I than that. Though I hesitate to focus too much on the death of Petronella Ottilia, it is not far-fetched to speculate that losing her so early might well have played a part in the decisions Melusine took later. Having such unbreakable bonds with her siblings meant she had always known the security that came with having a family to rely on. In allying herself so firmly to George Louis she maintained that sense of security not just financially, but socially too. The couple were so well-matched in temperament that Melusine's position was virtually – though not completely – unchallenged from the off, and it gave her back the rock-solid foundations that must have seemed to be crumbling when Petronella Ottilia passed away.

Baron von der Schulenberg eventually married again and embarked on a second family with his new bride, but this is no sorry tale of a wicked stepmother. In fact, the children of von der Schulenberg's second marriage were welcomed into the close-knit group that had already formed. Yet the von der Schulenberg children were all growing older and setting out on lives of their own. The boys entered the military[2], a natural berth for young men of such noble blood, whilst the girls were embarking on lives as wives and mothers. For Melusine, however, no suitors came calling. Though her family was well-respected, it was also far from unique or particularly special, and she was just one of innumerable, accomplished young ladies of marriageable age in Europe. There was little to distinguish Melusine from any other potential brides and unlike Sophia Dorothea, she was neither a princess nor in possession of a massive dowry and a future fat inheritance. If no likely husband came calling though, Gustavus Adolphus was certainly not about to keep Melusine at home forever. Instead, he fell back on his electoral connections and went searching for a position for his daughter that might expose her to eligible suitors, whilst at the same time providing her with a station of her own.

In 1690 he found it. Melusine was to travel to Hanover, where she would become a maid of honour to Duchess Sophia, wife of Duke Ernest Augustus. It was a substantial step up the social ladder and one that would, Gustavus Adolphus hoped, bring his daughter into the purview of a whole new selection of would-be bridegrooms. We must now leave Melusine behind for a little while. It's time to learn more about the world in which she was to flourish in Hanover.

---

2. Melusine's brother, Johann Matthias von der Schulenberg, enjoyed a highly distinguished military career well into his fifties.

The Electorate

If you wanted to reach the top in seventeenth century Europe, you had to be adept at all sorts of games. From war to diplomacy and everything in between, there was a lot to play for, and for ambitious rulers, the richest rewards were there for the taking.

One such ruler was Ernest Augustus, Duke of Brunswick-Lüneburg. Alongside his three brothers and fellow dukes, Christian Louis, George William, and John Frederick, Ernest Augustus ruled the Duchy of Brunswick-Lüneburg. The division of territories between the four brothers had led to a fractious and sometimes strained state of affairs and though each sibling hoped to one day be the man who would unite the lands of Brunswick-Lüneburg under one ruler, in the end that role fell to Ernest Augustus. The reason behind this was simple: Ernest Augustus was the only brother whose marriage produced a son and heir to inherit the duchy[3]. It helped that he was also a man of unfettered ambition who was happy to push his brothers aside to realise it.

Ernest Augustus' wife, Sophia of the Palatinate,[4] was a woman with plenty of ambition of her own. She was the daughter of the short-lived Frederick V, who was Elector Palatine until his death in 1623, and who ruled as King of Bohemia for just fifteen months. His tenure was so short that it earned him the nickname, *the Winter King*. Brief though his time in the spotlight was, Frederick's laurels paled in comparison next to those of his wife, Elizabeth Stuart. The Winter Queen had hit the dynastic jackpot: she had ancient royal blood flowing through her veins.

Elizabeth Stuart was the daughter of King James I and, like her eventual son-in-law, Ernest Augustus, she thrived on ambition. Elizabeth's own

---

3. Christian Louis died without issue whilst George William and John Frederick fathered only daughters. Girls were not able to inherit the duchy.
4. Sophia's remarkable life story can be read in my own book, *Sophia – Mother of Kings* (Pen & Sword, 2019).

marriage didn't go quite as she had hoped and instead of ruling a kingdom, as befit the daughter of a monarch, she ended up joining her husband in exile when the armies of the Holy Roman Empire banished the Winter King from Bohemia. The royal family left in such haste that they didn't even manage to pack all of the crown jewels and fled for a new life at The Hague without them.

Branded a yellow-bellied coward, the decline in Frederick's health and fortunes was swift. His lands were seized, his titles stripped from him, and he was left at the head of a powerless court-in-exile, from which he and Elizabeth made occasional abortive attempts to regain the favour of the Holy Roman Emperor and win back all that they had lost. Though the Palatinate lands and electorate would eventually be returned to the family after a fashion, Frederick didn't live to see it. Always subject to melancholy, he sank into a deep depression following the tragic death by drowning of his eldest son and never quite recovered from the shock. He died three years later of a fever, aged just 36[5].

Though Frederick was gone, his widow was far from beaten. From her exile in The Hague, Elizabeth Stuart indulged her love of politics and entertained visiting nobles from across Europe until her daughter, Sophia, observed that for all their illustrious visitors, "at our court we often had nothing to eat but diamonds and pearls"[6]. The family's coffers were as empty as its larders, but Elizabeth couldn't sell those diamonds and pearls, because they were vital to keeping up the illusion that a king's daughter needed to preserve. She had to look the part, even if she was starving.

When the monarchy in England fell and Elizabeth's brother, King Charles I, lost his head, the Protectorate understandably declined to offer any financial help to the exiled royal widow. Instead Elizabeth was cut adrift and, having come to rely upon wealthy royalists for support, found those sources of income were also now denied to her. In England, the estates and interests of her rich friends were being seized, leaving those

---

5. Intriguingly, Frederick's remains were disinterred from their resting place in Frankenthal by loyal friends when Spanish forces invaded. His body was taken to safety in the Sedan by Ludwig Philipp of Pfalz-Simmern-Kaiserslautern, but at this point it disappeared from the historical record. Today, Frederick's resting place remains a mystery.

6. Ward, Sean (trans.) (2014). *Memoirs (1630–1680)*. Toronto: Centre for Reformation and Renaissance Studies and ITER.

benefactors who had once lived in lavish style and funded the exiled court of the Winter Queen to join her in penury. Elizabeth surveyed her options and decided that there was only one thing for it. She set out to find a rich husband for her daughter, with all the steely determination of a general planning a military campaign.

Elizabeth's hope was that Sophia would snare Charles, Prince of Wales, and future king[7], but it wasn't to be. Though the prince came to The Hague and charmed the young lady, it soon became apparent that he had no interest in marriage. All he wanted was money, and that was the one thing that the exiled court couldn't offer him. So Charles went on his merry way and as belts tightened still further in The Hague, Sophia left her mother's side and travelled to Heidelberg, where she was to be a long-term guest of her brother, Charles I Louis, Elector Palatine, and his wife, Charlotte. It was during this trip that the young Winter Princess witnessed the damage that could be wrought by an unhappy marriage. She watched in horrified fascination as her brother and sister-in-law were alternately at war or in bed, their relationship *fiery* in all senses of the word.

Eventually the marriage of Charlotte and Charles Louis broke down irretrievably after Charlotte tried once too often to physically assault her husband's beloved mistress, Marie Luise von Degenfeld. After nearly biting through Marie Luise's finger and attacking her with a knife, Charlotte turned on Sophia, who she falsely accused of having an incestuous affair with Charles Louis. It was the final straw. The couple eventually divorced and Marie Luise was able to marry her man. It was a lesson Sophia would keep in mind when her own son's marriage began to bow under the weight of unfulfilled expectations.

It was at the fiery Heidelberg court that Sophia finally met the man who would become her husband. Charles Louis hosted a visit by George William and Ernest Augustus, two of the Dukes of Brunswick-Lüneburg, and she hit it off with Ernest Augustus from the start. Sadly, it seemed as though it had come too late. Charles Louis was actually in the midst of negotiating a betrothal between his sister and Adolph John I, Count of Zweibrücken-Kleeburg, brother of King Charles X Gustav of Sweden. The widowed count was noted for his unusual appearance, particularly

---

7. As King Charles II.

what Sophia described as a "long pointed chin like a shoehorn" and though she was in no hurry to become his bride, Sophia, Charles Louis and Elizabeth alike recognised that such a financially shrewd marriage might be enough to save the family from its hardships. The fact that Adolph John I was brother to a king was the cherry on top.

Terms for the Swedish marriage were still being discussed when much to everyone's surprise, George William of Brunswick-Lüneburg made a counter-offer. Just like Sophia's family, the party-loving duke needed money and the Hanoverian estates had agreed to award him a generous allowance on condition that he marry. He snatched Sophia from beneath Adolph John I's pointed chin and she was delighted. She far preferred the garrulous George William to her Swedish suitor and later recalled that when the proposal was received, "unlike the heroine of a novel, I did not hesitate to say yes"[8]. The marriage was on.

Yet even as Sophia was planning her wedding, George William was getting cold feet. No sooner had he secured the answer to his proposal than he received an unexpected increase in his allowance anyway, no marriage required. Now he could easily afford the lifestyle he wanted, and the last thing he needed was a bride to curb his fun. Unthinkably, George William offered to hand Sophia over to his brother, Ernest Augustus, which he reasoned would save Sophia from embarrassment as well as himself from any potential issues that might arise from this breach of promise. Ernest Augustus agreed to marry Sophia only on condition that George William would hand the wealthy territory of Lüneburg to him as well and would sign an undertaking in which he promised never to marry. The reason behind the second condition was that all-important territorial ambition. Ernest Augustus had plans for his lands and the last thing he wanted was George William fathering a son who might one day seek to regain Lüneburg for himself. George William accepted the deal and Ernest Augustus and Sophia were duly married. The bride herself was pragmatic. She had escaped the poverty-stricken deprivation of The Hague and "the only love I had felt was for a good establishment and that if I could obtain this I would have no difficulty trading the older brother for the younger"[9]. That's the spirit.

---

8. Ward, Sean (trans.) (2014). *Memoirs (1630–1680)*. Toronto: Centre for Reformation and Renaissance Studies and ITER.
9. Ibid.

The reason for this potted history of Hanover's rulers is to understand both the world in which Melusine was to flourish and the man she was to love. Duchess Sophia's origins were far grander than Melusine's, but she hadn't known the pampered, featherbed childhood of her daughter-in-law Sophia Dorothea either. Sophia had lived in genteel poverty, mixing with princes whilst her empty belly rumbled. She had lost a parent young and witnessed her brother's marriage being torn apart by infidelity and jealousies. She was acutely aware of her place in society and would do anything and everything to preserve and protect it. That included putting up with her husband's mistress because it was simply the done thing in royal marriages. George Louis learned about mistresses by following the example set by his father.

Sophia was 27 when she married Ernest Augustus in 1658. Two years later, she gave birth to her first son and heir, George Louis, the future George I. The spare, Frederick Augustus, came along the following year. Ernest Augustus had secured his line of succession. Now he needed to secure his claim to the territories that, by rights, should never have been his alone.

The dukes of Brunswick-Lüneburg had dreamed of seeing their duchy raised to the glittering status of an electorate ever since 1648, when the Holy Roman Empire made provision to admit new electorates to its rank. To be named an electorate was the highest honour a territory could receive and their rulers – the electors – were elevated to a status far above common-or-garden nobles. The electors alone were responsible for the election of a new Holy Roman Emperor when the current incumbent died and with that honour came power, prestige, and money. The rank of elector was symbolised by an electoral cap, or bonnet, and at a time when the Holy Roman Empire was still as powerful as it was vast, to be among the revered few electorates was every duchy's dream.

As the youngest of four brothers Ernest Augustus might have nurtured dreams of becoming an elector but realistically, he would have known his opportunities were limited. He would also have known that the Holy Roman Emperor would have balked at the very notion of letting four power-hungry siblings share an electoral cap. As long as the brothers divvied up their territories and responsibilities between them, Hanover would not be elevated any higher than it already stood. Only one man could rule over an electorate. Yet Ernest Augustus wasn't content to rest.

He had long since produced his heir and his spare when, in 1665, his eldest brother, Christian Louis, died. Christian Louis was followed by John Frederick in 1679 and suddenly, quite unexpectedly, fate had dealt Ernest Augustus a generous hand. He alone from the four brothers had produced an heir and though George William still lived, he had already promised never to marry. Out of nowhere, the prospect for the duchy's elevation to an electorate came once more into view.

Ernest Augustus had succeeded to the Prince-Bishopric of Osnabruck in 1662, under the terms of the Peace of Westphalia that decreed the office of Bishop should alternate between Catholic and Protestant holders. Ernest Augustus was the latter and with his new rank came a relocation to the bishop's residence at Iburg castle, which Sophia found dark, cramped, and dingy. In short, it was thoroughly ill-suited to the family's needs, so they set about constructing an opulent palace of their own in which to reside. After the deprivations of the exiled Winter Court, Sophia had had enough of being humble.

If Hanover was ever to become an electorate, it needed to look like one. Ernest Augustus was devoted to Italy – and its women – and adored the Venetian carnival. He envisioned Hanover as a *Venice of the North* that would rival the Italian city for romance and intrigue, and he was willing to spend serious money to achieve it. As well as the new construction at Osnabruck, Ernest Augustus' ducal residence at Herrenhausen and the family's ancestral castle, the Leineschloss, were both completely remodelled as part of the extensive programme of improvements. Herrenhausen in particular was seen by Ernest Augustus and Sophia as a showcase of Hanoverian excellence, and together they created a place worthy of any electorate. These renovations had been started by the late Duke John Frederick, but they now became Sophia's pet project. She nurtured the gardens and grounds of the estate and in her later years, they became a sanctuary in times of trouble. It was fitting, therefore, that Sophia would take her final peaceful breath on the grass of Herrenhausen's lawn decades later.

Hanover shimmered under the stewardship of Ernest Augustus. An annual carnival was established, and Venetians were brought into Germany to pilot ornate gondoliers along purpose-dug canals whilst musicians played on the shores and everyone who was anyone partied the night away. It was a must-see destination.

At first it seemed as though nothing could stand in the way of Ernest Augustus and Sophia's ambition. They had the land, they had the prestige, and they had the heir. All they needed to do was slot the last piece of the puzzle into place and approach the Holy Roman Emperor to make the first moves towards becoming the ninth electorate. But just when all was going smoothly, George William forgot the promise that he had made his brother years earlier. Not only did he fall in love, but he wanted to marry too.

Sophia first encountered Éléonore Desmier d'Olbreuse, destined to become a lifelong thorn in her side, when the exiled Huguenot had been serving as lady in waiting to the Princess of Tarente, a French noblewoman. Always one for the ladies, George William met Éléonore and fell for her just as he was about to undertake a trip to Italy with his brother and sister-in-law. He asked Sophia if she would bring Éléonore along on the tour ostensibly as a lady in waiting, but really it was so he could have his wicked way with her. Éléonore decided to remain with the Princess of Tarente, playing hard to get. She wouldn't play hard to get for long. Just like Melusine and Henrietta, her own illustrious career began as a lady-in-waiting in the circle of Sophia of Hanover.

Éléonore eventually came to Hanover once the trip to Italy was out of the way. She initially joined Sophia's household but was soon George William's official mistress, with a salary of 2,000 crowns per year to match. Though Sophia understood things had taken an intimate turn, she maintained her rigid adherence to protocol and, despite being the mistress of a duke, Éléonore was still treated as a servant by the duchess. She managed to secure herself the somewhat unimpressive title of *Lady Harburg*, (Harburg was part of the Hanoverian territories), but at mealtimes she was still seated at the staff table, whilst her plain supper wasn't half so enticing as the delicacies enjoyed by the dukes and duchess. What Éléonore wanted was the full works: marriage, a ring on her finger and the title of Duchess, just like Sophia. It's an indication of Sophia's absolute dedication to rank and protocol that she was determined to prevent Éléonore from getting her hands on either. She failed on both counts.

In 1666 Éléonore gave birth to Sophia Dorothea, who Melusine would one day supplant at court. It came as a surprise to everyone, since George William had long since been told that repeated bouts of venereal disease had left him unable to father a child. Instead he had somehow ended up with a mistress and a daughter who he adored, but he knew that if Sophia Dorotha was to stand a chance of fulfilling her marriage potential, she couldn't be branded as illegitimate. George William asked Leopold I, the Holy Roman Emperor, to legitimise his union with Éléonore. When Sophia heard that George William had approached the emperor she was outraged, but Ernest Augustus was a little more pragmatic. He needed the Holy Roman Emperor on side if Hanover was to become an electorate and he reluctantly agreed to support George William's audacious request. Sophia was disgusted, referring to Éléonore scathingly as a "little clot of dirt", but she was powerless to stop the Holy Roman Emperor from legitimising the marriage. She was equally powerless to prevent her newly minted sister-in-law from parading triumphantly through Celle in her state carriage, or to stop George William from buying up the rich territory that surrounded his existing lands. Ernest Augustus' agreement with his brother might initially have left George William worse off, but now the situation was in sharp reverse.

In Celle, George William enjoyed the benefits of land and money, as well as the PR boost afforded by a popular wife and a pretty daughter. That daughter was growing into an eligible young lady, and as wealthy families with unwed sons jockeyed for position, Duchess Sophia took matters into her own hands. As far as she was concerned, there could only be one man who would make a suitable bridegroom for Sophia Dorothea.

"[George Louis is] the most pig-headed, stubborn boy who ever lived, and who has round his brains such a thick crust that I defy any man or woman ever to discover what is in them," said his mother, but that didn't deter her from doing everything in her power to ensure George Louis became the bridegroom of his cousin, Sophia Dorothea of Celle. It was a masterful decision to pursue a marriage that would ensure the vast wealth of Celle that Sophia Dorothea stood to inherit would one day flow into Hanover's coffers. By marrying the cousins, there was also no chance that Sophia Dorothea would wed an ambitious outsider who might agitate for his own slice of the Brunswick-Lüneburg fortune. Yet Sophia would have to wait for an answer, because George William wouldn't even entertain the notion of his daughter's marriage until she turned 16.

This, of course, is a book about two particular mistresses, but one mistress at Hanover far outstripped all the others. She also brought Melusine von der Schulenberg into the heart of the Hanoverian court.

Clara Elisabeth von Meysenburg and her sister, Catherine Marie, were the pretty and accomplished daughters of Count Georg Philipp von Meysenburg, an impoverished adventurer. When his efforts to make a splash with his girls at Versailles failed, he took them instead to Hanover, where they stood out as they never had in the glamourous French court. The sisters shone at a gala in 1673, when they dressed as romantic shepherdesses and performed a short sketch for Ernest Augustus. Soon after, they married George Louis' governors, Franz Ernst von Platen and Johann von dem Busche, and Clara took her place among Sophia's ladies-in-waiting. She was nearly 20 years Sophia's junior and Ernest Augustus quickly made her his official mistress, whilst her sister slipped into bed with his son George Louis. Between them, the two young ladies had snared both the duke and his heir.

Catherine Marie was not George Louis' first *amour*. In 1676 the young man became a father for the first time when an affair with his sister's under-governess resulted in pregnancy. The nameless young lady had come with Sophia from her brother's Heidelberg court and Ernest Augustus feared a scandal, but instead her family spirited both mother and baby away. Money almost certainly changed hands to buy their silence and the mother and child were spoken of no more. Ernest Augustus was glad to see his son take Catherine Marie as a lover in place of the under-governess. She understood the role of a courtly mistress and could be relied upon to be discreet.

Clara's presence and influence over Ernest Augustus made Sophia miserable, but she knew better than to make a scene. Instead she bore her husband's infidelity without complaint and indulged in petty acts of revenge, such as forcing the heavily made-up and overdressed mistress to join her on long, brisk walks in the summer sunshine. As Sophia glided through the gardens, Clara laboured in her wake, sweating and exhausted. Clara took her own sort of vengeance when both women delivered sons in 1674, each calling them Ernest Augustus. Clara's husband claimed the little boy as his own son, and everyone dutifully looked the other way. Like all courts, Hanover was one in which a mistress wouldn't raise so much as an eyebrow, but a pregnant mistress could cause all sorts of problems.

Yet Clara, unlike Melusine, was absolutely clear in her motivations. She wanted power above all else. Thanks to her machinations her husband eventually rose to the rank of prime minster, and nobody exercised more unofficial influence at court than she did. Years later that influence would lead to murder. It would also prove instrumental in bringing Melusine into Sophia's circle.

In 1682, on the very eve of Sophia Dorothea's sixteenth birthday, Sophia of Hanover leapt into a carriage and raced through the night to her brother-in-law's castle at Celle. She knew that her son had at least one rival for the wealthy princess' heart and she was determined to be the first on the scene. She arrived early enough to catch George William dressing and Éléonore sleeping and, by the time her social climbing sister-in-law awakened, the deal had been done. Sophia Dorothea would marry the surly, disinterested George Louis. She would bring with her a fortune in dowry and with the two cousins married, the territories of Brunswick-Luneburg would be reunited. What had once been divided between four brothers might soon stand to be inherited by one lone son: George Louis.

Famously, when the young princess was told that she was to marry her cousin, George Louis, she retorted furiously, "I will not marry the pig snout!", but marry him she did and she was expected to make the best of it. George Louis simply accepted the union as his fate, recognising that his father's ambitions for the future of the family were more important than any wishes that he might have. Hoping to give the new couple the best start they could hope for, Sophia even banished George's mistress, Catherine Marie von dem Busch, before the bride-to-be arrived in Hanover. George Louis would greet his new wife with an empty bed.

George Louis and Sophia Dorothea married on 22 November 1682. Their first child, who would one day rule as George II, was born within a year and their second, a daughter named Sophia Dorothea, came along in 1686. Though this might appear to suggest a happy or at least tolerable marriage, the reality was far different. Yet as things began to unravel in the relationship between the couple, in the government of Hanover, all was going from strength to strength.

Like his father, George Louis was a born soldier. It was a time when continental warfare was rife and for the victor, the pickings could be rich. Shrewd politicking and some fierce battles had seen Ernest Augustus' star gradually rise over the years and Hanover's with it, but there remained the question of inheritance. Ernest Augustus had two children by his mistress, Clara, but these were acknowledged by her husband as his own and had no place in the line of succession. The same couldn't be said for his official children.

The matter of succession would have been relatively simple if George Louis had been the only son of Sophia and Ernest Augustus but instead the couple were extraordinarily fecund. Setting aside the traumatic miscarriages and stillbirths that Sophia suffered, they still raised seven children to adulthood. All but one of them were sons. Even given the fact that George William was father only to a single daughter, that meant the lands that had once been split between four brothers now faced an even worse fate: to be split between six. If that happened, Ernest Augustus might as well kiss his dreams of a glamorous electorate goodbye.

The answer was obvious. The six-way split simply wouldn't work, so an alternative had to be found. Ernest Augustus began to investigate the possibility of passing on the estates and titles of Hanover via primogeniture, simply meaning that there would be no divide in future generations, but that the eldest son would inherit everything. He could see no other way forward and following the marriage of George Louis and Sophia Dorothea, began to make the necessary arrangements for the change. The ducal family knew nothing of Ernest Augustus' decision until Emperor Leopold had agreed it, but still there was no guarantee that Hanover would ever be an electorate. Leopold, however, was under siege. The massed forces of France were beating at the doors of the Holy Roman Empire and Ernest Augustus' well-drilled armies were a valuable part of the Empire's defence. In time, the military support Ernest Augustus could lend to the emperor would prove too valuable to ignore. The road to the electorate was becoming ever smoother.

In 1684 Ernest Augustus announced to his family that from now on, primogeniture would be the method of Hanoverian succession. The decision shook the ducal court to its very roots, and nobody was more furious than Frederick Augustus, the second son of Sophia and Ernest Augustus. His protests grew so angry that Ernest Augustus eventually threw him out. Years later when Frederick Augustus died in battle it was the turn of the third son, Maximilian William, to realise that primogeniture had robbed him of what could have been a very lucrative opportunity indeed. He conspired to overthrow his father and was eventually thrust into exile too, narrowly escaping execution. Some of his co-conspirators weren't so lucky. George Louis didn't only learn about mistresses by his father's example. Ernest Augustus also taught him that dissent in the family wasn't to be tolerated and if one's sons proved problematic, they could simply be banished. George Louis would certainly follow that example to the letter.

Whilst Melusine was growing into a young lady at her father's castle in Emden, dreaming of what the future might hold and where the world might take her, she could little guess that events not only in Hanover but far away across the sea would one day make her a quasi-queen, uncrowned but far from unknown.

As Ernest Augustus hustled at home in 1688, in England the Glorious Revolution changed the political landscape forever. At its heart was religion. King James II had converted to Catholicism in the late 1660s and though the move was unpopular, it hadn't quite sparked a revolt until he baptised his newborn son, James, Prince of Wales, into the Catholic faith too. At the thought of at least another generation of Roman Catholic rule, a group of well-connected Protestant nobles known collectively as the Immortal Seven, decided that a change was due. James II's Protestant daughter, Mary, was married to William III, Prince of Orange, and the Immortal Seven wrote to him and invited him to come to England and usurp the king. If he agreed, the nobles could offer military backup and the promise that the people of England would throw their support behind the coup. It was an audacious move.

As William and his armies sailed for England, Louis XIV offered James II France's military support. The beleaguered monarch fatefully declined, believing that he was more than equipped to see off the Orange invasion. He was to be proven wrong and, when William and his army made landfall in November 1688, James realised that he'd made a catastrophic mistake. Protestant soldiers amongst his own ranks defected to the Orange cause and James' daughter, the future Queen Anne, joined forces with those who sought to dethrone her father. Yet William preferred a bloodless takeover and he allowed James to escape to France. There he remained in exile until his death, never able to regain the crown he had lost.

In England, William and Mary took their place on the throne with their position enshrined by the Bill of Rights, which established the new constitution. It was also time to think about succession, as the new sovereigns had no children who would succeed them. Although Anne was the next in line, she would produce no living heirs despite over a dozen sometimes traumatic pregnancies. Though nobody knew it yet, this meant that the line of succession would eventually skip fifty Roman Catholic claimants to the crown and land on the next Protestant in line. That Protestant was Sophia of Hanover.

Of course, with Anne only in her twenties and happily married to a man she loved, the chance of Sophia succeeding ahead of any children the young princess might yet have was scant indeed. Ever the pragmatist, Ernest Augustus considered the possibility of his wife ever inheriting the English crown so remote that he barely even considered it. Instead he focussed all his efforts on the vacancy in the Holy Roman Empire for a ninth electorate, a vacancy he was now closer than ever to filling.

When the Palatinate War broke out between the Holy Roman Empire and the French, it was the might of Hanover that held the balance. From both sides, envoys bearing gifts and promises trekked to the Leineschloss, each hoping to win Ernest Augustus to their cause. Ernest Augustus promised France and the Holy Roman Empire that he would consider both options but true to form, he was hustling again. "[There is] great talk of creating a new Elector in favour of the Duke of *Hanover*," wrote the English press, "Never had that Most Serene Family a more favourable Opportunity; but 'tis much to be fear'd that the Prince will meet with Obstacles, and that all Endeavours will be us'd at *Rome*, to dissuade the Emperor from it."[10]

But Ernest Augustus was ready to take up the cudgels and emerge as the victor. The duke approached the electors and assured them that he would be willing to send Hanover's armies into battle on their behalf if they formally supported the elevation of the duchy to an electorate. With French armies poised to land a damaging blow, the electors of the Holy Roman Empire consented to admit Hanover to their select number. Though there would be years of negotiation to secure the final honour, Leopold had no choice but to bow to Ernest Augustus' demands. He desperately needed military help and only Ernest Augustus could provide

---

10. *Present State of Europe or the Historical and Political Mercury.* 1 May, 1692.

it, so the deal was done. Hanover was to become the ninth electorate of the Holy Roman Empire[11], and George Louis was its sole heir.

It was in this duchy on the edge of greatness that Melusine von der Schulenberg was to make her mark.

---

11. Hanover was officially recognised as an electorate in 1692 and Ernest Augustus received his longed-for electoral cap the following year in a characteristically showy ceremony.

A New Arrival

Just as Count Georg Philipp von Meysenburg had taken his daughters first to Versailles and then to Hanover in search of opportunities, so too did Gustavus Adolphus, Baron von der Schulenberg, tread a similar path. He had no need of French favour though, for he already enjoyed the patronage of the Elector of Brandenburg and with such patronage came wealth, influence and a name that meant something. For Ernest Augustus, there could be no better recommendation. His only daughter, Sophia Charlotte, had married the elector[12] in 1688, and he had enthusiastically championed his Hanoverian father-in-law's efforts to raise his duchy to the status of an electorate ever since. Any friend of Brandenburg could count themselves a friend of Hanover too and it was amongst these friends, especially the most rich and powerful of their number, that Gustavus Adolphus hoped that he might find a husband for his as yet unmarried daughter.

Melusine arrived at a time when marital relations between George Louis and Sophia Dorothea were in steep decline. With their heir and spare safely delivered the ill-matched husband and wife had grown more distant than ever, and the lonely Sophia Dorothea had renewed her acquaintance with a childhood friend, Count Philip Christoph von Königsmarck. George Louis was brooding and bad-tempered, and he was concerned with little beyond the military and his future prospects. Sophia Dorothea was bored, spoilt and desperate for romance. It was hardly a surprise when the couple fell apart.

Clara von Platen, meanwhile, was still sitting pretty at the side of Ernest Augustus. She rued the removal of her sister from the court not because she missed her company, but because she resented the fact that she had lost her hold over the son of the house. For that she blamed Sophia

---

12. Frederick and Sophia Charlotte later became the first king and queen in Prussia.

Dorothea[13], and she fully intended to restore her influence by bringing Catherine Marie back into the fold. When Catherine Marie was widowed it looked like fate had dropped the perfect opportunity into Clara's lap, but George Louis no longer had any interest in his former mistress. What had seduced him as a young and single man held no excitement for the married and worldly soldier he had become.

When Melusine and her father arrived in Hanover, they were keen to make their presence felt on the social scene. How better to make a splash than by lodging at Monplaisir, the opulent residence of the socially dominant von Platens? Monplaiser glittered even more than the palaces of Hanover and the festivities that Clara hosted there were as lavish as anything Duchess Sophia could achieve and twice as notorious too. She revelled in her position as mistress, even if she was forced to be subservient to Sophia to achieve it, but the duchess was as stately and disinterested as the mistress was shrewd and ambitious. It was only a matter of time before Clara von Platen wove her web around Melusine.

It was Clara who introduced Melusine to Sophia and recommended her as a lady-in-waiting. Mindful of Melusine's connections to her daughter's Brandenburg court and her excellent pedigree, Sophia agreed, and the strikingly tall and thin, blue-eyed young lady joined the inner circle of the electress-in-waiting. Whilst it's possible that Melusine was complicit in Clara's scheme to install her as the mistress of George Louis, it's unlikely. She had not come to Hanover looking for a lover, but for a stable future, and for a woman of Melusine's background marriage was a far more wholesome prospect. Should she become a mistress her future marriage prospects would be indelibly dented. For now at least, she was the virginal incomer from an unremarkable if pretty town. She was just 22 years old and boasted a well-connected family, so Melusine's chances of making an excellent match were high. Instead, she took a different path.

How it happened is a mystery but Melusine and George Louis were lovers within months of her arrival and nobody was more surprised than his mother. Taciturn, undemonstrative, and frankly rather short, George Louis made a somewhat comical sight at the side of his tall, unfashionably skinny companion. Clara doubtless played a part in introducing the couple,

---

13. The murderous tale of Sophia Dorothea, Count von Königsmarck, and Clara von Platen can be found in my book, *The Imprisoned Princess* (Pen & Sword, 2020).

but there was really nothing that unusual in a lady-in-waiting taking the dual role of mistress. Sophia wasn't impressed. During a ball she turned to Henrietta Howard, the second subject of this book, and crowed, "Look at that tall mawkin and think of her being my son's passion!". Not only that, but now Sophia had a double embarrassment to contend with on a day-to-day basis. It wasn't only her husband who had a mistress amongst her ladies-in-waiting, but her son too.

Socially things had fallen out of balance, but George Louis and Melusine were well-suited despite the obvious physical differences. Sophia Dorothea was emotional and quick to lose her temper, whereas Melusine was placid and patient and soon learned that discretion was the way to a happy life with her lover. She and George Louis were far more suited in personality and interests than the warring husband and wife ever were. Melusine and George Louis loved to ride out and hunt, whilst Sophia Dorothea far preferred the glitz of a ball or gala. Her pampered childhood had taught her that she should always be number one, yet somehow Melusine had effectively supplanted her in the affections of her husband and everybody at court knew it. It was humiliating.

Though often portrayed by her detractors as a dull, pliant creature, Melusine was far from it. She was certainly not "little above an idiot,"[14] as her own son-in-law would have us believe. George Louis' granddaughter, Wilhelmine, was a little kinder to her grandfather's amour and wrote that, "The Duchess of Kendal was a good woman. She had no great faults or great virtues,"[15] which is certainly a rather more balanced character appraisal than those of some of her detractors. In fact, Melusine was intelligent, thoughtful, and quietly influential. In the battle between Melusine and Sophia Dorothea, she was simply the more suitable candidate to partner the electoral prince.

---

14. Stanhope, Philip Dormer, Earl of Chesterfield (1777). *Characters of Eminent Personages of His Own Time*. London: William Flexney, p.10.
15. Christian of Schleswig Holstein (1887). *Memoirs of Wilhelmine, Margravine of Baireuth*. New York: Scribner & Welford, p.40.

The Family

Whilst George Louis and Melusine were getting closer, his relationship with Sophia Dorothea was falling apart. For Clara, who was delighted that her favoured candidate had filled the vacancy for a mistress left by her sister, things couldn't have gone better. All that was left was to seal the deal.

Catherine Marie returned to Hanover to celebrate her marriage to a Hanoverian general with a party hosted by her sister, Clara. Upon learning that George Louis and Melusine intended to attend the party as a couple, Clara invited Sophia Dorothea along too, revelling in the knowledge that the crown princess would be utterly humiliated to arrive alone and witness her husband and his mistress leading the dancing. In the event and much to Clara's chagrin, Sophia Dorothea was taken ill and couldn't attend. For the rest of the gossip-hungry court the dance between the couple served as confirmation that George Louis and *La Schulenberg* were very much official. Among those courtiers was Sophia Dorothea's confidante, Eleonore von dem Knesebeck, who passed word of the relationship on to her devastated friend. As a final nail in the coffin, whenever George Louis visited the Leineschloss he made his home not in his marital apartments, but in those occupied by Melusine. She was already edging Sophia Dorothea out of the picture, simply by her presence.

It's worth mentioning here Sophia Charlotte von Platen, another important woman in the life of George Louis. Sophia Charlotte was George's half-sister via Ernest Augustus' extra-marital liaison with Clara von Platen and she had inherited her mother's penchant for making trouble. Just as Melusine would one day be mocked as the *Maypole*, Sophia Charlotte would come to be known in England by the unflattering moniker of the *Elephant*, thanks to her enormous bulk. Years later, the splendidly waspish Horace Walpole remembered her thus:

"[Sophia Charlotte], whom I saw at my mother's in my infancy, and whom I remember by being terrified at her enormous figure, was as corpulent and ample as the Duchess [Melusine] was long and emaciated. Two fierce black eyes, large and rolling beneath two lofty arched eye-brows, two acres of cheeks spread with crimson, an ocean of neck that overflowed and was not distinguished from the lower part of her body, and no part restrained by stays – no wonder that a child dreaded such an ogress, and that the mob of London were highly diverted at the importation of so uncommon a seraglio!"[16]

Court rumour had it that Sophia Charlotte was George Louis' mistress either just before Melusine came on the scene or at the same time. Since she also happened to be his half-sister, the rumours of intimacy were more than simply scandalous. Gossip about her supposed incestuous intrigue with George Louis grew so widespread at the Hanoverian court that the mortified Electress Sophia stepped in and put a stop to it once and for all. Despite those scurrilous whispers amongst courtiers, George Louis and Sophia Charlotte remained friends throughout their lives. She married in 1701 and her husband, Johann Adolf von Kielmansegg, was immediately welcomed into the elector's inner circle, a state of affairs that left Melusine ruffled. Alongside her sister-in-law, Sophie Karoline von Platen, Sophia Charlotte was one of the sharpest thorns in Melusine's side for many years and she was as blunt as her rival was diplomatic. When George Louis travelled to England, the battle between Melusine and Sophia Charlotte to be the first woman to join him was to cause even more trouble for the mistress. George Louis' granddaughter, Wilhelmine, echoed the thoughts of many when she decided that Sophia Charlotte was "very clever, but used her cleverness to no good purpose, and was a slave to evil ways."[17] In those ways, one might say that she was her mother's scheming daughter.

Though it was virtually a given that royal men would take a mistress, they were expected to do so on the understanding that such an arrangement would cause their wives no embarrassment. By dancing and cavorting with

16. Walpole, Horace (1798). *The Works of Horatio Walpole, Earl of Orford: Vol IV*. London: GG and J Robinson, p.285.
17. Christian of Schleswig Holstein (1887). *Memoirs of Wilhelmine, Margravine of Baireuth*. New York: Scribner & Welford, p.40.

Melusine at a public occasion such as Catherine Marie's party, George Louis had flouted the one rule he was expected to obey. The *mawkin* was now more of a companion to George Louis than Sophia Dorothea had been for years and the crown princess was determined to avenge her errant husband. She did so by taking as her lover the dashing adventurer, Count Philip Christoph von Königsmarck, but she reckoned without his love of the spotlight. When Königsmarck regaled high-ranking friends at the court of Dresden with tales of "a prince [who would] destroy the life and happiness of his good and beautiful wife by neglecting her for an impudent and worthless mistress", gossip soon spread across the Empire about the trouble at the heart of Hanover. Inevitably, word of the count's pointed comments reached Melusine and George Louis. Königsmarck had crossed the line.

The result was catastrophic. George and Sophia Dorothea argued like never before and when Sophia Dorothea challenged him about his relationship with Melusine, George Louis attacked her. He threw her to the floor and would have choked her were he not physically dragged away by Sophia Dorothea's attendants. Duchess Sophia spirited Sophia Dorothea off for a restorative break, whilst George Louis remained in Hanover where Melusine could soothe his troubled brow. Though Clara von Platen would spend the next years scheming against Sophia Dorothea and Königsmarck, who had once been *her* lover and had thrown her aside for the unhappy crown princess, Melusine had no such ambition and certainly none of the jealousy that drove Clara. Melusine had come to Hanover seeking security and though the position of a mistress was sometimes precarious, it was still better than nothing. George Louis' favour gave her protection, prestige, and an easy life, and unlike Clara she had no ambitions to influence the electoral court's future and no political axe to grind. Perhaps most important of all, Melusine certainly had no personal dislike for Sophia Dorothea, the woman whose husband she now accompanied everywhere. Instead she had simply seen an opportunity for advancement and had taken it. Such was life in Hanover.

After the birth of Sophia Dorothea of Hanover in 1686, there were to be no more children for the crown prince and princess. Truth be told, as relations between them deteriorated to the point of violence, there was probably precious little intimacy too. The same certainly couldn't be said for Melusine and George Louis.

Tragedy struck in October 1691 when Melusine's father, the very man who had brought her to Hanover and decided her future, died. The family had always been close, and his loss hit Melusine hard. Though she was an adult by the time she was orphaned, the security offered by George Louis now became more important than ever. Melusine was still grieving for the late Gustavus Adolphus when she gave birth to her first child the following January. In the cries of the newborn infant no doubt she took some comfort and joy after the long, hard winter. All Melusine and George Louis' children were girls and the parents named their firstborn Anna Luise Sophie, known as *Luise*. Unlike George Louis' other illegitimate child, this time the mother wouldn't be paid off and asked to leave Hanover for good.

Melusine had not been present when the unfortunate undergoverness and child were banished from court and it's highly likely that she knew nothing of it. Though courtiers loved to gossip, to spread rumours about the heir to his adored mistress would not have been a wise move. Perhaps Melusine even expected that her lover would acknowledge their daughter, and all would proceed as normal. If that was the case, she was to be sorely disappointed.

When Sophia Dorothea learned of the little girl's birth she was humiliated and angry. She confronted her husband about the baby and once again, things turned violent. George Louis rounded on Sophia Dorothea and attempted to strangle her. Unsurprisingly, their relationship would not recover from this second brutal assault. From that point on, George Louis concentrated on Melusine.

Ernest Augustus had had two illegitimate children of his own with Clara von Platen, but her husband had happily claimed paternity of them in exchange for favours and promotion, despite the fact they never had any biological children of their own. This might seem extraordinary, but it was simply the way things were done, so it will come as no surprise to learn that George Louis once again followed his father's example and declined to acknowledge Luise as his own. It was Melusine's first brief brush with the kind of public humiliation to which George Louis had treated Sophia Dorothea, and she was entirely unequipped to deal with it. The court of Hanover was her whole world and she had gone from the crown prince's acknowledged favourite to the unenviable position of an unmarried lady-in-waiting with a baby. It didn't matter that the father was the heir to the electorate, to be an unwed mother could still spell social death for Melusine. Something must be done to save her reputation.

Yet Melusine was not the scheming and wrathful Clara, nor was she Sophia Dorothea, who felt so abandoned in her marriage. What she had that neither of those women did was a large, loving and close-knit family, and it was they who offered Melusine a helping hand in her most dire hour of need. It was so close-knit, in fact, that when George Louis was looking for two trusted men to join his household, he chose Melusine's brothers, Friedrich Wilhelm and Johann Mattias. Both went on to enjoy highly celebrated military careers thanks to their sister's court connections. The family looked after its own and it would look after the newborn baby girl too.

Though little Luise continued to live in Hanover with Melusine, she was officially acknowledged as the child of Melusine's elder sister, Margarete Gertrude, and her husband. It set a precedent and in time, all three children of Melusine and George Louis would be formally acknowledged as the offspring of Melusine's siblings. When a second daughter, Petronella Melusina, was born the following year, she too was acknowledged as the daughter of Margarete Gertrude. Melusine's youngest sister, Sophie Julianne, would acknowledge Melusine and George Louis' third and final child, Margarethe Gertrud, as her own in 1701. The von der Schulenbergs knew how to close ranks when they had to.

This was the best possible outcome for everyone. It was especially fortuitous in the case of the first two children, who came along at a time when George Louis' marriage was in crisis and the House of Hanover was in the process of celebrating its elevation to an electorate. Although George Louis didn't acknowledge paternity, he didn't intend to ignore his children either. The arrangement with the von der Schulenberg siblings meant that he was able to see his second family freely without embarrassing Hanover at the moment of its greatest triumph. It was the perfect solution.

An Electoral Divorce

As the 1690s wore on, George Louis barely saw his wife if he could help it. He spent much of his time away on military campaigns and when he was at home, every free moment was occupied by Melusine. She entertained him every evening in her chambers, where she made satirical paper-cut caricatures of courtiers as her beloved songbirds trilled on their perches. Sometimes she joined the crown prince on trips away whilst at home, Sophia Dorothea alternated between rage, boredom, and despair. The only chink of light on the horizon was the promise of a new life with Königsmarck, if only they could escape Hanover together. An elopement could be disastrous for the electorate in more ways than one. Not only would it be embarrassing, but should the lovers find sanctuary with one of Ernest Augustus' enemies, it could be politically costly too. For Clara, it was just one more way to make mischief. She impressed upon Ernest Augustus the importance of preventing the couple's rumoured elopement, stressing the instability a rogue crown princess could cause in the region. He consented to have Königsmarck arrested, but his mistress went much further than that. Her actions would have shocking consequences for the marriage of George Louis and Sophia Dorothea, and subtly changed the status of Melusine forever.

On the night of 1 July 1694, as Königsmarck left Sophia Dorothea's rooms in the Leineschloss, he was attacked by four armed men in the pay of Clara von Platen. It was she who dealt the killer blow, kicking her former lover in the mouth as he took his dying breath. Only then did reality hit and the panicking killers disposed of their victim's remains and tried their best to cover up the crime. The body of Königsmarck has never been found. When Sophia Dorothea awoke on the morning of the planned elopement, she was immediately placed under house arrest. As the missing count's sister searched the Holy Roman Empire for any trace of her brother, Melusine was the shoulder on which George Louis could lean. He lost no time in refusing Sophia Dorothea any further audiences with her children and to her dying day, she never saw them again.

To the horror of Ernest Augustus, the goings-on at the Leineschloss were soon the talk of polite society across the empire. George Stepney, William III's envoy in Dresden, wrote to James Cresset, the British envoy in Hanover, hungry for all the gossip and keen to share his own take on the unfortunate situation.

> "I have great curiosite to know what piece of mischief has been brewing at Hanover. If you dare not trust it at length, I must beg you to satisfy me in Cypher, as likewise with the particulars of your Princess's ruine. [...] A servant or two of Count Königsmarck run frequently betwixt this place and Hanover [...] seeking out their master, but have no tidings. [...] I have been told his sister [Aurora] raves like Cassandra and will know what is become of her brother; but at Hannover they answer like Cain, that they are not her brother's keeper and that the Body should be found [...] I knew [Königsmarck] in England, at Hamburg, in Flanders, and at Hanover for a dissolute debauchee whom I would always have avoided. [...] This is all I have had to do with the spark, and if he has been as black as we think he is, his Fate (be what it will) is not to be pitied."[18]

When Sophia Dorothea was questioned about her role in the affair by Count von Platen, Clara's far from impartial husband, she maintained her innocence. Perhaps surprisingly, George Louis was still willing to forgive his wife at this point, if only to save the new electorate any further embarrassment. He informed Sophia Dorothea via Baron von Platen that she would be freed from captivity and returned to her rightful place at his side if she swore to be an obedient wife from that day forwards. The very idea of this sickened her and Sophia Dorothea replied loftily that "if what I am accused of it true, I am unworthy of his bed; and if the accusation is false, he is unworthy of me. I will not accept his offers."[19]

---

18. Stepney to Cresset, *Dresden Despatch*, 24 July–3 August 1694.
19. Coxe, William (1798). *Memoirs of the Life and Administration of Robert Walpole: Vol I*. London: T Cadell, Jun, and W Davies, p.469.

Sophia Dorothea had sealed her own fate. If the couple couldn't live together, then they would be divorced. Sophia Dorothea was condemned to genteel confinement in Ahlden House on the river Aller, where she remained until her death more than three decades later. The day after the divorce was finalised, Hanover held one of the greatest carnivals the electorate had ever seen. As wine flowed and fireworks lit up the night sky over the stately gondoliers, Melusine von der Schulenberg was the only woman at George Louis' side.[20]

---

20. Following the death of Königsmarck, Clara von Platen swiftly discovered that she had brought about her own disgrace too. Once the most powerful woman at court, she was swept up in gossip about the missing nobleman and had to endure Ernest Augustus' fury at her blatant disregard for his instructions. Clara became ever more isolated and eventually succumbed to syphilis, which left her blind and disfigured. William Makepeace Thackeray fancifully claimed that Königsmarck's ghost tormented the agonised countess as she lay on her deathbed, sending her mad before she took her final breath on 30 January 1700.

The Act of Settlement

In January 1698, Ernest Augustus, Elector of Hanover, died. Thanks to his hard-headed decision to bring in primogeniture, his title and territories were inherited by his eldest son, the now divorced George Louis. Though he was now Elector of Hanover, it wasn't until 1701 that the Act of Settlement set George Louis' future and that of Great Britain in stone. The act ruled that the line of succession to the English and Irish crowns could only be occupied by Protestant heirs, with no exceptions. With only William III, Princess Anne, and the Electress Sophia now standing between him and the throne, it was almost a foregone conclusion that George Louis would one day reign in England. He would do so with no queen at his side, for Melusine was in no way a suitable wife for a man who had been raised as George Louis had, no matter how much he loved her or how loyal she was. Few royal mistresses ever made it to the altar to marry their patrons.

Often dismissed as cold and unloving, in fact George Louis could be quite the opposite when the mood took him, but it required very specific circumstances to bring out his warmer side. He didn't like to be challenged and he hated being laughed at, as proven by his enraged attack on Sophia Dorothea when Königsmarck mocked Melusine at the Dresden court. Melusine, however, was something of a natural diplomat. Maybe it was because of the security she felt in her role, or perhaps it was the fact that, unlike Clara, she really only sought an easy life and wasn't interested in gaining power and leverage. Whatever the reason, Melusine was a lady who people seemed to like. Not for her Countess von Platen's furious scrabble for scandal. Instead it seemed to nobles such as her future son-in-law, Albrecht Wolfgang, Count von Schaumburg-Lippe, that Melusine sought only "to do all the good she can". Simplistic, perhaps, but that might go some way to explaining how she held the top spot beside George Louis for as long as she did. A reign of more than three decades was not to be sniffed at.

Yet with Sophia Dorothea confined to Ahlden and her name forbidden at court, it was the placid Melusine who still sat at George Louis' side, wife or not. Together they spent their leisure time not in the palaces where George Louis' former wife had once paced and fretted, but in a brand new, purpose-built hunting lodge at Göhrde. The couple's new sanctuary cost more than 80,000 thalers and was designed by George Louis' court architect, Louis Remy de la Fosse, and Johann Christian Böhm. The lodge became one of the most magnificent buildings in the region and was particularly celebrated for its hunting parties, whilst in the evenings, guests could enjoy performances in its private theatre. It was a secluded haven for the couple, and they escaped to Göhrde whenever they could.

Though he might not have been the sort to shout about it, George Louis needed Melusine more than ever in 1705 when his sister, Sophia Charlotte of Hanover, died unexpectedly of a ruptured stomach. George Louis was bereft, and his mood was hardly helped by his frosty relationship with his own son, George Augustus. The young man had been unable to forgive his father for having Sophia Dorothea imprisoned at Ahlden and the bad feeling would seethe for years, driving a wedge between the two for as long as George Louis lived. Though things between the elector and his heir were tense, George Louis enjoyed far easier relationships with his legitimate daughter Sophia Dorothea and the children he shared with Melusine. By this time they were parents to three daughters, all of them claimed by Melusine's siblings but each loved by their true parents even if their real paternity wasn't acknowledged. The court of Hanover had become a family home once more.

George Louis and Melusine's three daughters were well-known and well-liked figures at court, but it was Gertrud, who was known by all as *Trudchen*, who was by far her father's favourite. She was a spirited and tomboyish girl who often accompanied George Louis on hunting parties and nursed dreams of one day becoming a soldier. Her gender meant that those ambitions could never be realised and instead Trudchen flourished as one of the favourites of the Hanoverian court, as celebrated for her sparky character and lively nature as she was for her good looks. Whether she considered a life at court a fair substitute for serving in the military is, of course, unconfirmed.

Just as George Louis had his favourite amongst his children, so too did Melusine. She had a particularly strong bond with Petronella Melusina, who was known to all as Young Melusine. Just like her mother, the inoffensive Young Melusine served as a maid of honour to Electress Sophia and was as gently unassuming as Trudchen was enthusiastic and sociable. Young Melusine would be her mother's constant companion through the decades to come, continuing to stay by her side even after her own marriage.

In many ways the lives of the three girls were considerably easier than those of George Louis' legitimate children precisely because they had no official standing. There was no rush to find royal husbands for the three illegitimate girls but in the case of Luise, the eldest of the trio, that lack of urgency in making a dynastic marriage led the family into trouble. When she was just 15, Luise asked her mother and father for their permission to marry Ernst August Philipp von dem Bussche-Ippenburg, a senior officer in Celle's military and a member of a highly influential family. It wasn't what her parents had hoped for but despite their reservations, they eventually acquiesced to her repeated demands. Unfortunately the marriage was not a happy one, and by 1714 the couple had parted ways thanks to Luise having "had a thousand lovers, and [being] catched in bed with a man [and] been divorced from her husband upon it."[21] Never one to bite his tongue, the gossipy Baron Hervey even accused Luise of having an affair not only with George I – her father, let's not forget – but with his son, George II, and *his* son, Frederick, Prince of Wales. "Which was one generation more," he noted waspishly, "than the Duchess of Valentinois could boast of in France."[22] It's safe to say that there was no truth in that allegation. Unfounded rumours of incest just seemed to follow George Louis around.

The lack of official acknowledgement for the girls was of particular importance to the Dowager Electress Sophia, who valued rank and propriety above most things. She had lobbied the late Ernest Augustus long and hard for the right to bring her own nieces and nephews to Hanover after the death of her brother, Charles Louis, Elector Palatine, and each time he had refused, citing the difficulties their presence might cause when it came to precedence between them and George

21. Croker, John Wilson (ed.) (1848). *Memoirs of the Reign of George II from his Accession to the Death of Queen Caroline by John, Lord Hervey: Vol II*. London: John Murray, p.126.
22. Ibid., p.100.

Louis' children – illegitimate or otherwise. This, along with Melusine's original position as a humble lady-in-waiting, did nothing to improve her standing in Sophia's eyes. She would never acknowledge Melusine as anything other than her inferior no matter how long she remained at the side of George Louis. Decades might pass but for the Dowager Electress of Hanover, time served was no substitute for rank. Instead Sophia would always regard Melusine as the *mawkin*, an inoffensive figure to be tolerated at best and mocked at worst. It didn't matter how much George Louis loved Melusine or how steadying her influence was, let alone how good a mother to his children she might be, the Dowager of Hanover would never warm to *La Schulenberg*.

The King's Mistress

"Letters from Hanover of the 8th of this Month bring an Account of the Death of the Princess Sophia Electress Dowager, Mother of the present Elector. Her Highness being walking in the Garden of Harrenhausen [sic] between 6 and 7 in the Evening of the Day, was seized with a sudden Illness, and sunk down as in a fainting Fit, but expired before she could be carried into her Apartment."[23]

The Dowager Electress of Hanover was 83 years old when she expired in the gardens of her beloved Herrenhausen. From the moment that the phlegmatic Sophia became a frontrunner in the line of succession, she never really believed that she would live long enough to take place on the throne, much as she wished she might. In fact, she was right. Sophia of Hanover died on 8 June 1714 and less than two months later, on 1 August, Queen Anne of Great Britain followed her to the grave. Exhausted by illness and over a dozen pregnancies that ended in tragedy, the late queen's body could bear the strain no more. Great Britain was about to change forever.

"It having pleas'd Almighty God to take to himself Our late most Gracious Queen of Blessed Memory, We Hope, that nothing had been Omitted, which might Contribute to the Safety of these Realms, and the Preservation of Our Religion, Laws, and Liberties, in the Great Conjecture. As these Invaluable Blessings have been Secured to Us by those Acts of Parliament, which have Settled the Succession to these Kingdoms in the most Illustrious House of Hanover.

[…]

---

23. *Daily Courant*. 5 June, 1714; issue 3936.

Preparations are making for the solemn Funeral of her late Majesty, and if they can be ready soon enough 'tis said she will be interred before the King's Arrival."[24]

As the population waited for King George I to arrive from the continent, some fretted about the threat from Scotland, where James Francis Edward Stuart, *the Old Pretender*, was poised to press the Jacobite claim to the throne. Others held their breath, fearing exactly what this change in the status quo might bring when the family from Hanover arrived. Still others celebrated the end of the old regime and the beginning of the new, ready to embrace the future and profit from it as handsomely as possible. It was a time of unknowns for everyone, not least King George I.

The new king was about to enter an arena unlike any he had known and a world away from the absolutist electorate of Hanover. He was coming into a political landscape that was riven by factionalism, where the Tories and the Whigs stood either side of the battle lines and neutrality was not an option. Despite this, George Louis intended to favour neither and instead planned to appoint the best candidates for office regardless of political persuasion, but the shrewd Whigs had already done the groundwork required to position themselves as the pro-Hanoverian party. In the event when George Louis appointed his first British cabinet, he stuffed it full of Whigs. Within months of his arrival in the kingdom, they were the ruling party.

History has dismissed Melusine von der Schulenberg as obsessed not with power, but with cash. If Robert Walpole was to be believed, "money was with her the principal and prevailing consideration," but whether that was really the case is open to question. As the divorced king's mistress Melusine certainly enjoyed a level of privilege that few could dream of, and there were precious few to whom she must bow and scrape, as Henrietta Howard was forced to do. Yet claims that she was "so venal a creature, that she would have sold the king's honour for a shilling advance to the best bidder,"[25] scarcely take into consideration not only the privilege of Melusine's life at the side of George Louis, but its precarious state

---

24. *Daily Courant*. 7 August, 1714; issue 3990.
25. Coxe, William (1816). *Memoirs of the Life and Administration of Sir Robert Walpole: Vol I*. London: Longman, Hurst, Rees, Orme, and Brown, p.151.

too. Melusine had no safety net. Should her companion tire of her or decide to trade her in for a younger candidate, as happened frequently in the hothouse world of the European courts, she had little to cushion her fall. During her long relationship with George Louis there was frequent gossip that he had other lovers, but one in particular is worth mentioning.

Sophie Karoline von Platen was the wife of George Louis' illegitimate half-brother, Ernst August von Platen, and a great favourite of George Louis. As a Catholic she was set aside upon his accession to the Protestant British throne and the threat she posed to Melusine's position was removed, though she would return to cause trouble later. Yet despite her rivals Melusine remained the most senior female in Hanover, even though her dominance relied on George Louis' continued affections. When the new monarch set off for his new kingdom her settled existence came under siege as never before. For the first time, it seemed likely that Melusine's grip on her patron might be fatally weakened.

It wasn't a rival who threw Melusine for a loop though, but the dramatic change of lifestyle and location that she was about to face. Melusine had been left without a mother at a young age and that loss had cemented the bond between the von der Schulenberg children. They became her closest friends and she repaid their friendship and loyalty with money, honours, and rank. Upon coming to Hanover she could have held out for a husband, for it's likely a woman of solid breeding and excellent familial connections like Melusine would have found one. Instead of waiting though, she had taken the hand of George Louis and with it came no permanent guarantees.

When George Louis inherited the British crown, it meant a wholesale move to England for not only the new king, but more than one hundred German courtiers and household staff too. By the terms of the Act of Settlement no German candidate could hold official office in Great Britain, but George Louis intended to get around this by appointing his German favourites as advisors rather than officials. Though the German contingent technically had no power, in reality they had lots of it. After all, it wasn't merely for *advice* that George Louis relied on Baron Andreas Gottlieb von Bernstorff, one of Hanover's most senior politicians and a long-time conspirator of Clara von Platen. The baron had once been Prime Minister of Celle and in England he continued virtually unchecked, riding roughshod over British ministers, and wielding huge influence over the new monarch. Baron von Bernstorff was a political fly in the ointment for the British.

Only one person had more access to the king than von Bernstorff by the time the Germans set sail for England. That was Melusine, but if she was to maintain her position, it would mean leaving the only home she had known for twenty years. In Hanover she had raised her daughters and risen to the top of the pecking order little by little simply by enduring, but now she faced the challenge of uprooting her foundations to journey to a country that wasn't even certain that it wanted the Hanoverians. It was a journey that Melusine wasn't sure that she was willing to undertake.

George Louis left Melusine behind in Hanover, keen to get to England and relieve the temporary Regency council of their duties as soon as possible. Having prepared for the job for years, he was ready to rule. His sea journey was difficult and dangerous and Melusine initially demurred and remained in Hanover, leading Lady Mary Wortley Montagu to sneer that Melusine did so "fearing that the people of England, who, she thought, were accustomed to use their kings barbarously, might chop off his head in the first fortnight; and had not love or gratitude enough to venture being involved in his ruin."[26] It might make for a good joke, but there was no truth in it.

In fact, Melusine's reluctance to leave Hanover was likely far more to do with the fact that she had made her home there for decades than a fear that the British might be about to lop off the new king's head. Those who later sought to make her a figure of grotesque comedy claimed that when Melusine was faced with the possibility of moving to England, she responded by running wild laps of the gardens at Herrenhausen, embracing the statues and trees and frantically declaring that nothing could possibly induce her to leave her beloved home. Yet this seems at odds with the placid Melusine, who merely longed for a place of her own. Melusine's mind was made up. She would not leave Hanover for England, no matter how much her lover begged.

George Louis' triumphant accession to the British throne was no doubt tarnished by his mistress' refusal to join him in his new realm, but he could delay no longer, and he left as soon as the weather allowed. However,

---

26. Wortley Montagu, Lady Mary (1817). *The Works of the Right Honourable Lady Mary Wortley Montagu, Vol III*. London: R Bentley, pp.164–165.

no sooner had Melusine made up her mind to remain in Hanover than she changed it again, and all it took was a bit of old-fashioned jealousy. George Louis' half-sister and rumoured mistress, Sophia Charlotte von Kielmansegg, announced that she was planning to accompany the royal retinue to England, knowing that Melusine would not be there to keep her from holding total sway over George Louis. Though Sophia Charlotte's debts made it difficult for her to leave Hanover and George Louis didn't offer to pay them – hardly a ringing endorsement of her company – she fled the electorate in disguise and sailed by night for the new kingdom. That was enough to prompt Melusine into action and she packed her bags and left the electorate behind to give chase before Sophia Charlotte could get her feet under the table. She and the couple's three daughters – ostensibly Melusine's nieces – braved treacherous seas to arrive just a short time behind George Louis. She had narrowly averted disaster.

Though fluent in French, the language of European royalty, Melusine had already begun learning English too, which she hoped would stand her in good stead at the British court. She mastered the language with far more willingness than her lover ever showed. Though he certainly could understand English when the mood took him, George Louis preferred to stick to German. His ambition wasn't to make friends, it was to rule. He wanted to establish the House of Hanover in Britain and banish any doubts about the German incomers once and all. This wasn't a time for social niceties, but for action.

For Melusine, meanwhile, what mattered was re-establishing a home. At first, she was content to linger in the background and to try to be as anonymous as possible until George Louis was settled, mindful of the fractious public mood and the need to keep an already tense situation under control. It's testament to this that George Louis accepted the advice of courtiers that Melusine shouldn't attend his coronation. They warned that making a mistress part of such a solemn occasion would send the wrong messages, further inflaming those who already questioned the legitimacy of the Hanoverian claim to the throne.

When George Louis learned that his coronation had been attended by other former royal mistresses, he was far from happy that they had witnessed what his own mistress could not. Melusine would linger in the background no longer. She and the couple's daughters swiftly joined George Louis and his court at St James's Palace, where they found their accommodation damp and dark, but there was to be no programme of renovation like that undertaken at Herrenhausen by George Louis' parents. What work was carried out on the palace by the dour sovereign was strictly necessary to ensure their comfort, but it stopped short of luxury.

This wasn't the case at Kensington Palace, which eventually became the couple's favoured British home. During his reign, George Louis had a vast amount of work carried out by William Kent that completely transformed Kensington Palace and can still be seen and admired today. He had a purpose-built wing added specifically to house Melusine and she became so attached to the place that it was a wrench when she had to give it up for a new home following her companion's death. Kensington Palace subsequently became home to George II and his own family, not to mention his mistress, Henrietta Howard, who found that George I's renovations didn't stop a crop of mushrooms from growing up through the floor of her chambers. Royal splendour at its finest.

When it came to housing, Melusine was far from exempt from criticism. In fact, she was about to taste the blunt reality of being a British king's mistress. When Sir Christopher Wren was dismissed from his long-held position as Master of the King's (previously Queen's) Works in 1718, there were those who pointed the finger of blame for his sudden departure at Melusine. According to them, the king's mistress had demanded several unsympathetic changes be made to the royal palaces and insisted haughtily that Wren obey her every whim. When he resisted her architectural mutilations, her critics claimed that Melusine had him unceremoniously kicked out and replaced by her personal choice of William Benson. In fact, the truth is likely rather more mundane than that. When Wren left his position, he was 85 years old. By anyone's standards, retirement at such an advanced age is hardly likely to raise any eyebrows, yet we shouldn't let Melusine entirely off the hook here. She certainly did clash with Wren on the matter of the royal residences and it's impossible to be sure that her imperious side didn't come out a little when she did. Her annoyance at Wren, combined with his Tory leanings, would certainly have done him no favours in the eyes of George Louis. It wasn't wise to upset the king's mistress.

Though Melusine had her daughters at her side as she attempted to navigate the waters of her new court, she had reckoned without the bitter opposition of the Tories and their supporters. In their eyes, George Louis was a usurper and the women who came with him were as bad if not worse. A particularly savage and bestselling pamphlet entitled *Upon the Thanksgiving Day* captured perfectly the fury reserved for the king and his entourage.

> "The Golden Age is now at last restor'd!
> *ANNE* is no more; but *GEORGE* is *Britain's* Lord!
> Now Justice, Plenty, Joy, & Fortune smile
> With *GEORGE's* Genius on this happy Isle.
> Peace go with *NAN*: In her what have we lost?
> Or what has *GEORGE* to these three Kingdoms cost?
> Nothing, when weigh'd with what by him we've got,
> And wheat from *Herrenhausen* he has brought,
> Here he hath brought his dear Illustrious House,
> That is, himself, a Close-stool, & a Louse;
> Two *Turks*, three Whores, and Half a Doz'n Nurses,
> Five Hundred *Germans* all with empty purses."

The woman who had spent so many unobtrusive years in Hanover was now branded a whore, regarded with disgust and suspicion for the simple fact that she wasn't the wife of the king. George Louis' coronation, where it was wrongly claimed that "Kielmansegg and Schulenburg [sic] with their ruddied cheeks [stood] grinning behind the Defender of the Faith,"[27] was greeted by riots and the new monarch hit back hard, invoking the Riot Act and either arresting protesters or impeaching the nobles amongst them. It was a messy affair all round, but George Louis was unbowed. In fact, the grotesque image of the grinning Maypole and ruddied Elephant were unfounded. They were certainly not standing behind George I as he took his solemn oath, but that wouldn't make such a good story.

Melusine slotted into life in St James's Palace just as quietly as she had in Hanover. The palace was far from luxurious but she made the best of it,

---

27. Thackeray, William Makepeace (1816). *The Four Georges*. London: Smith, Elder and Co., pp.39–40.

and that placid manner that had worked in Germany was soon brought to bear in England too, but Melusine was no soft touch and she wasn't afraid of going after what she believed she deserved. She even managed to turn the cold, damp palace to her financial advantage, successfully making a case for an increase in her fuel, refreshment and lighting budgets on account of the fact that the king himself spent each evening in her chambers. For that reason alone, Melusine argued, she couldn't be expected to entertain him without the budget to keep the candles lit. Placid she might be, a pushover she was not.

Whilst the newly arrived Prince and Princess of Wales became beacons of fashionable society and public popularity, for the king there was to be no such adoration. George Louis had been dour in Hanover and now he was dour in London too, maintaining his privacy as far as he could and balking at suggestions that he should follow his son's example and work on becoming a man of the people. He had no qualms about Melusine carrying out whatever social engagements she chose in her efforts to fit into her new life, but he did not wish to be part of them. The glamour of the Wales' household held no appeal for King George I.

What was apparent from the moment George Louis arrived in his new realm was the fact that he had transported much of his familiar German world with him. The household of the late Queen Anne was suddenly filled with the acolytes of the incoming Hanoverians – among them Henrietta Howard, as we shall see later – and there were naturally fractious interactions with the two sides, each clamouring for power and influence in the new administration, whilst simultaneously attempting to reach a harmonious living arrangement. Yet mockery met them at every turn, as the two cultures clashed in the throne room and the drawing room alike.

"Countess of *Buckenburgh* said, in a Visit, that the English Women did not look like Women of Quality, but made themselves look as pitifully and sneakingly as they could; that they hold their Heads down, and look always in a Fright, whereas those that are Foreigners hold up their Heads and hold out their Breasts, and make themselves look as great and stately as they can and more nobly and more like Quality than the Others. To which Lady *Deloraine* replied, "We show our Quality by our Birth and Titles, Madam, and not by sticking out our Bosoms.'"[28]

Between Germany and England, there was a constant battle for court supremacy that would persist for years. Despite this, in day-to-day terms Melusine's life as the king's favourite was little altered. It's no wonder that Lady Mary Wortley Montagu's sharp nib was able to skewer the monarch and his mistress so easily.

"[Melusine] was so much of [George Louis'] own temper that I do not wonder at the engagement between them. She was duller than himself, and consequently did not find out that he was so; and had lived in that figure at Hanover almost forty years (for she came hither at threescore) without meddling in any affairs of the electorate, content with the small pension he allowed her, and the honour of his visits when he had nothing else to do, which happened very often."[29]

When she wasn't enjoying quiet nights in with George Louis, Melusine spent her days making her social calls or in church. She worshipped several times a day according to some correspondents, who wryly speculated that she did so in the fear of what fate might otherwise await her in the hereafter, having served as mistress to someone else's husband for so many years. Yet in the here-and-now, little had changed for the couple. They still passed their evenings in quiet companionship and Melusine still entertained George Louis with caricature silhouettes as he smoked at her side, just as she had in Hanover. Though not given to displays of affection, Horace Walpole later wrote that George Louis had promised Melusine that she would never be without him even after death, and it's true that they were closer than the king and his ill-fated wife had ever been. He dined with his mistress and their daughters most evenings and it was implicitly recognised that they were a family, rather than an unmarried couple taking supper with their nieces.

---

28. Cowper, Mary (1865). *Diary of Mary Countess Cowper, Lady of the Bedchamber to the Princess of Wales, 1714 -1720*. London: John Murray, p.102.
29. Wortley Montagu, Lady Mary (1837). *The Letters and Works of Lady Mary Wortley Montagu, Vol I*. London: R Bentley, p.93.

Sometimes Melusine and George Louis went to the theatre, where the king preferred to eschew the spotlight and sit behind Melusine in the box allotted to the Maids of Honour, out of sight of the public. Often they both kept out of the limelight, leaving George Augustus and his wife Caroline to champion the celebrity lifestyle. Though she had her familiar and trusted circle of Hanoverian ladies, Melusine also made a concerted effort to widen it to include the wives of senior and influential English courtiers, but just as she had at home, she kept out of politics. At first, that is.

As with any long-term relationship things weren't always rosy and Melusine took a particular dislike to George Louis' boozy afternoons with Robert Walpole. After the men had been out on a hunt they lolled around chatting and getting drunk, smoking their pipes as they set the world to rights. Melusine didn't approve of these scenes of conviviality because she was far from fond of the politician's influence over her patron, but she was wise enough to not to interfere too openly. She secretly asked her fellow German courtiers to try and break up the party but instead they poured a drink, lit a pipe, and joined in. Melusine took it on the chin. Besides, after two decades as the unassuming, brow-soothing mistress of George Louis, her loyalty was about to be rewarded.

Titles and Rivals

> "His Majesty has been pleased to create Erengard Melosine [sic].
> Baroness of Schulenburg [sic], a Baroness, Countess, Marchioness
> and Duchess of Ireland, by the Name, Style and title of Baroness of
> Dundalk, Countess and Marchioness of Dungannon, and Duchess
> of Munster."[30]

In 1716 Melusine was naturalised as a British citizen. George Louis
rewarded her loyalty with the title of Duchess of Munster, along with
payments to the tune of several thousand pounds a year. When the Duke
of Somerset resigned as Master of the Horse that same year, instead of
appointing a new candidate to the post and paying them the £7,000
annual salary that went with it, it was paid to Melusine instead. Though
she was generous with her family to a fault, the new Duchess of Munster
certainly didn't live humbly. In the Georgian era cash was king, opening
doors and heaping status onto whoever held the purse strings. To thrive
at court, you needed money, and Melusine knew that more than anyone.

Cash attracted criticism and followers in equal measure and Melusine
was never short of company, as courtiers jostled to be near to the woman
who sat at the king's right hand. Though she didn't initially meddle
in political affairs, ambitious social climbers knew that one word from
Melusine during her nightly meetings with the king could do more
than hours spent bowing and scraping in the throne room. Even as the
chattering classes smiled and tugged their forelocks, they were rather
sniffy about the German incomer, as Lady Cowper's recollections of
overheard gossip at a court function suggests.

> "[Lady Cowper commented] "there was a good deal of music, yet
> I could not avoid being uneasy at the repetition of some words

---

30. *Post Man and the Historical Account*. 3 July 1716–5 July 1716; issue 11250.

in French which the Duchess of Bolton said by mistake, which convinced me that the two foreign ladies [presumably Schulenburg and Kielmansegg] were no better than they should be".[31]

Nicknamed "the Maypole" by the public on account of her height and build and dismissed as no better than she should be by the very courtiers who flocked to fill her apartments and win her favour, Melusine was nevertheless immovable. She enjoyed money, titles, and privileged access to the sovereign, but what made her an attractive prospect also made her a target. There was always someone else who wanted what she had and like all royal mistresses, Melusine quickly learned that it paid to stay alert. On top of ambitious social climbers, there was no shortage of would-be replacement mistresses either. George Louis might have kept Melusine at his side, but that didn't mean that he didn't have a roving eye and Caroline of Ansbach's maids of honour certainly wrote knowingly of his tastes. When Margaret Bradshaw told Henrietta Howard that "the king has a new bird out of my neighbourhood, which I hear he is very fond of", the suggestion that George I wasn't above taking supplemental mistresses alongside Melusine rang loud and clear. There would always be "a new bird" to catch his eye. Like any long-suffering royal wife Melusine mostly put up with that roving eye without complaint, but when it roved towards Mary Lepell, she sat up and took notice.

Known as Molly by all at court, Mary Lepell was a well-connected young lady who, at the age of 15, was appointed maid of honour to Caroline of Ansbach, George II's future queen. Molly had all the qualifications for advancement at the Georgian court. Bright, bubbly, and beautiful, she was determined to make her mark.

"She was extremely forward and pert," wrote the Duchess of Marlborough to Horace Walpole, and those qualities rather recommended her to the king. Upon her birth, the young woman had been made a cornet in her father's regiment and though it was an honorary appointment, it brought with it a salary that was very real indeed. Once Molly became a maid of honour she moved to cement her status, correctly guessing that her honorary military salary might not be paid for much longer. Thanks

---

31. Wilkins, WH (1901). *Caroline, The Illustrious: Vol I*. London: Longmans, Green, and Co., p.177.

to her charms, "my Lord Sunderland got her a pension of the late King, it being too ridiculous to continue her any longer an officer in the Army", and the one-time cornet left her rank behind. With her military pension and her *pertness*, Molly soon became of the most notorious ladies at court, despite her youth. George Louis couldn't have failed to notice her.

Molly was so celebrated a beauty that poets fell over themselves in their efforts to memorialise her best qualities. Even Voltaire asked of her, "Would you know the passion, You have kindled in my breast?", but Voltaire was merely one in a long line of admirers, with George I at the head. Well-versed in the games of court intrigue, Molly seemed to pose a genuine threat to Melusine's position, and it was obvious to all. For years George Louis had enjoyed nightly appointments with Melusine but now Molly and George Louis were together each evening instead, albeit at drawing rooms with other courtiers present. Once the king had left the gathering Molly mockingly repeated everything he had told her to her friends, revelling in being the centre of attention. Amongst those friends was Caroline of Ansbach's gossipy and scheming favourite, John Hervey, 2nd Baron Hervey of Ickworth, who had something of an interest in Molly himself.

Fearing that Molly's mocking indiscretion and love of the Prince of Wales' set might prove dangerous, Melusine eventually paid her rival £4,000 to make herself scarce. Molly subsequently married Lord Hervey and continued to be as notorious as she was celebrated for nearly five more decades. Melusine had seen off one rival, but there were others. There always would be, right until the end of the king's life.

Politically aware if not particularly active, Melusine, Duchess of Munster, owed her new Irish title to her friendship with Charles, 2nd Viscount Townshend, who was Secretary of State for the Northern Department. He was the brother-in-law and close political colleague of the infamous Robert Walpole, who wielded enormous influence and power as First Lord of the Treasury and Chancellor of the Exchequer. Melusine was far from fond of Walpole, who called her "as much Queen of England as ever was", but he recognised how important she was in keeping the king on side. A highly intelligent and shrewd politician, Walpole made use of Townshend's friendship with Melusine wherever possible. As Baron Hervey noted, "the Duchess of Kendal never loved Sir Robert Walpole, and was weak enough to admire and be fond of Lord Townshend, [and] the canal of application had always been from Lord Townshend to the Duchess and from the Duchess to the King."[32] The importance of the royal mistress could not be downplayed. Perhaps that was the reason that Walpole stood by without complaint and let his own wife share the king's bed from time to time.

Lord Townshend secured the title of Duchess of Munster for Melusine in the belief that she would be delighted with it and ready to reward him handsomely. At first she was, but her excitement didn't last once she realised that the grand-sounding rank didn't carry anything like the cache of an English peerage. The Act of Settlement denied the king the right to award English peerages to the Germans, but Melusine had been naturalised and it rankled that a more prestigious title could have been hers. In a world in which favours were a fact of life, Townshend had fatally undervalued Melusine's price. He was swiftly demoted to the lesser role of Lord-Lieutenant of Ireland and after just four months in that post, he was dismissed.

Though Townshend was sure that Melusine had orchestrated his downfall out of spite, this might not have been entirely true. The viscount had other enemies, not least Charles Spencer, 3rd Earl of Sunderland, and James Stanhope, who was to become 1st Earl Stanhope. Despite a long and enduring business relationship with Hanover that had existed since the reign of Queen Anne, when George Louis came to the throne Sunderland had been forced to settle for the surprisingly lowly office of Lord-Lieutenant of Ireland. He was determined to claw his way back to the top of government and a matey trip to Hanover in the company of the king transformed the fortunes of both Sunderland and Stanhope, at the expense of their mutual opponents, Townshend and Walpole. Though Melusine was certainly annoyed at her relatively meagre Irish honour, it was Sunderland and Stanhope who convinced George Louis that Townshend and Walpole had been conspiring against him with the Prince of Wales, and George Louis' immediate recourse was to demote Townshend accordingly. On the day after Townshend was dismissed from Ireland in 1717, Robert Walpole resigned. Of course, he would later rise to the very pinnacle of government.

---

32. Croker, John Wilson (ed.) (1848). *Memoirs of the Reign of George the Second: Vol I.* Philadelphia: Lea and Blanchard, p.135.

Though the Stanhope-Sunderland pairing was undoubtedly at the root of Townshend and Walpole's troubles, Townshend was convinced that upsetting Melusine had been his biggest mistake. In a letter he railed against the reasons that had been given for the hobbling of his career, acknowledging that, "[Sunderland] directly charges the lord chancellor, my brother Walpole, and me, with having entered into engagements with the prince [of Wales] and form'd designs against the king's authority."[33] Yet, after a long and detailed description of the many and varied ways in which he had been insulted by Sunderland, Townshend closed the letter by dismissing it all as so much hogwash. Instead, he levelled the blame at the Hanoverian contingent, who made easy scapegoats for a disenfranchised British statesman. Baron von Bernstorff, it must be said, was certainly a man given to the sort of Machiavellian schemes that could end a career, but whether Melusine would have been so enraged at her Irish peerage that she orchestrated Townshend's dismissal in revenge is open to question.

> "These are all the reasons I have yet heard alledg'd for my disgrace. [...] However, though these are the topics given out by my enemies, I am far from thinking that they are the true and originall [sic] causes of my disgrace. I believe the duchess of Munster, Mr. Bernstoff [sic] and Mr. Robethon[34] could give a much more exact and authentic account of the real causes that produced this event, if they thought it as much for their own service, as it might be for my credit to have the whole mystery of this alteration laid open."[35]

Melusine was fast learning the political ropes. In Hanover, the first lady of the court was the late Electress Sophia, who made sure to keep Melusine in her place no matter how close she and George Louis might be. It was in England that Melusine was able to come into her own and flourish, disproving those earlier court biographers who dismissed her as an idiot

---

33. Coxe, William (1798). *Memoirs of the Life and Administration of Sir Robert Walpole, Early of Orford: Vol II*. London: T Cadell, Jun. and W. Davies, p.161.

34. John Robethon was secretary to George Louis. He was close to Sunderland and disliked Robert Walpole.

35. Coxe, William (1798). *Memoirs of the Life and Administration of Sir Robert Walpole, Early of Orford: Vol II*. London: T Cadell, Jun. and W. Davies, p.162.

who grabbed at money and jewels, with little in her head beyond avarice. She disliked Walpole from the off and Townshend was tarnished by his closeness to the First Lord, so the fall of both of them was of little consequence to her but besides this, Stanhope and Sunderland's role in toppling their political opponents was far more significant than that of the king's mistress. Walpole and Townshend *had* been paying close court to the Prince of Wales, so they were already on shaky ground and their enemies were quick to capitalise on it.

Yet when a Prussian envoy wryly noted that Melusine was often the person who "broke the first ice" when it came to winning an audience with the king, he wasn't wrong. Breaking the first ice via Melusine could be a shrewd political move, and she could apparently work miracles with the king too. Nobody would learn that better than the Prince and Princess of Wales when a domestic explosion shook the royal household to its roots and caused a rupture at the heart of the court.

When George Louis and his son, George Augustus, came to England together in 1714, their relationship was already strained. It wasn't helped by the fact that George Augustus' seven year old son Frederick stayed in Hanover, where he was to act as the ceremonial figurehead of the family. This meant he was in regular correspondence with his grandfather and whilst George Louis undertook trips back to the electorate to see his grandson, George Augustus didn't meet Fred again for more than a decade. As young Frederick fell more and more under the influence of George Louis, the domestic situation in England grew increasingly tense. The two Georges had virtually nothing in common and whilst the king's subjects regarded him as a dour and rather unappealing figure, the Prince and Prince of Wales were beloved celebrities, whether glittering at the theatre or even, in the case of George Augustus, heroically extinguishing fires and keeping London and its people safe.

Melusine soothed her companion's brow through all his domestic trials and was at his side when he developed the symptoms of an anal fistula in September 1717. The same ailment had struck down Louis XIV in 1686 and tales of the agonising and dangerous surgery he endured were still told, so George Louis was terrified by the prospect of having to endure similar treatment. For Melusine, this was a dose of reality. It was the first time she had been forced to really face the fact that she might lose her companion and she was worried at the prospect of what looked like an uncertain future. Without the king, she hardly knew what might await her. Happily, George Louis' fears were to prove unfounded and the eventual diagnosis was one of haemorrhoids. For now, Melusine would keep her king.

The relief at court was immense but short-lived, for another drama was brewing and even Melusine couldn't prevent the eventual estrangement of father and son. It began in 1716 when George Louis refused to appoint George Augustus as his regent whilst he was out of the country visiting Hanover. The Prince of Wales felt the insult deeply, but their festering mutual dislike finally came to a head in 1717 when a row erupted over the christening of the Wales' newborn son, George William, and the king's insistence on the Duke of Newcastle as godfather. George Augustus was so inflamed at his father's meddling that a scuffle broke out at the christening, during which Newcastle claimed that the Prince of Wales had challenged him to a duel. The prince hotly denied the allegation, but George Louis chose to believe Newcastle.

In a situation that calls to mind Ernest Augustus cutting off his own dissenting sons in Hanover, George Louis banished his heir from St James's Palace and issued an order that any courtiers who continued to see George Augustus would likewise be banished. Caroline of Ansbach had not been exiled but when she chose to follow her husband to his new lodgings at Gloucester House, the king refused to let her take their children with her. All of them, including the newborn George William, were to remain at St James's in their grandfather's custody. The split was bitter and, for the parents who were forced to leave their youngsters behind, it was heartbreaking.

Caroline pined for her children desperately and the canny Walpole, sensing a way to get the Prince of Wales into his debt, suggested that she approach Melusine and ask if she would speak to the king on her behalf. It did the trick. George Louis relented and agreed to grant Caroline access to her children, though he flatly refused to allow George Augustus the same privilege. Only when Prince George William fell dangerously ill did his grandfather relent and grant George Augustus permission to visit the children and say one last goodbye to his youngest son. George William died at just three months old, leaving his family bereft.

At least Caroline and George Augustus could find some peace in the knowledge that their youngsters were being treated well. Melusine was never malicious and she viewed her partner's family as an extension of her own. Thanks to the close bonds between her and her siblings in childhood, she knew better than anyone that youngsters needed affection to flourish without the presence of their parents. Affection was something George Augustus had singularly lacked after his mother had been taken away, and the consequences of that separation could be seen in every tortured argument and clash between father and son. Though Melusine was certainly motivated by money on occasion, cruelty for its own sake held no interest for her and she considered George Louis' grandchildren her own. She made it her business to keep the youngsters happy despite the forced absence of their parents and their lives were a long way from that of George Augustus, who had been forbidden from even mentioning his own mother's name. Melusine had a maternal instinct that made her a natural caregiver for the children and to her, there was no distinction between step-grandchildren and the real thing. She made sure that the youngsters were always given rooms near to her own, so that there was always a friendly face to turn to. She loved them like a grandmother and they in turn found comfort in her presence.

At Gloucester House, the Prince and Princess of Wales sat at the head of an alternative court that was filled with George I's political opponents. Chief among them was the Machiavellian Robert Walpole, who enjoyed a long and enduring friendship with Caroline that proved valuable to both when she was crowned queen. Indeed, it was he who eventually negotiated a shaky peace between father and son that endured until the former's death. Despite this, George Louis never quite trusted Walpole, but he knew that it was better to call him an ally than an enemy. Melusine, on the other hand, had more pleasing matters to deal with for now.

"His Majesty has been pleased to create Her Grace Erengart Melusina Dutchess [sic] of Munster, a Baroness Countess and Dutchess of Great-Britain, by the Name and Style and Title of Baroness of Glastenbury [sic] in the County of Somerset, Countess of Eversham in the County of Kent, and Dutchess of Kendal in the County of Westmorland."[36]

---

36. *Weekly Journal or British Gazetteer.* 9 May 1719.

When Melusine was given the all-important title of Duchess of Kendal in 1719, it was a tacit acknowledgement of her importance in George Louis' life and her influence over him. What she wanted, she got, and as Townshend and Walpole learned, it was never a good idea to incur the wrath of this usually quiet and unassuming woman. Melusine and George Louis' daughter, Luise, was honoured with the title of Countess of Dölitz[37], whilst Sophia Charlotte von Kielmansegg, Melusine's nearest rival if not for the king's affection then at least in terms of feminine influence, would have to wait years for a similar honour[38]. Unlike Molly Lepell, those who wanted a more subtle kind of leverage knew that the path of least resistance was to make Melusine a friend rather than have her as a foe. She spoke English fluently and was happy to receive English courtiers, unlike George Louis who preferred to stick to German, was uneasy in social situations and didn't make new friends easily. Nobody was closer to the king than the Duchess of Kendal, so it made sense to kowtow to her if one hoped to join the innermost circles of the sovereign.

"As the Duchess of Kendal seemed to express a wish to see me often, I have been very attentive to her, being convinced that it is highly essential to the advantage of your Majesty's service to be on good terms with her, for she is closely united with the three ministers who now govern,"[39] wrote Count de Broglio, the French envoy in London, to Louis XV. A veteran of Versailles and its dizzying life of intrigue and court protocol, he had sussed out the lie of the land in Great Britain with no trouble whatsoever.

"The King visits her every afternoon from five to eight; and it is there, that she endeavours to penetrate the sentiments of his Britannic majesty, for the purpose of consulting the three ministers, and pursuing the measures which may be thought necessary for accomplishing their designs. She sent me word, that she was desirous of my friendship, and that I would place confidence in her. I assured her, that I would do every thing [sic] in my power to

---

37. Luise received her title thanks to a piece of property that was owned by the von der Schulenberg family. Their second daughter, Young Melusine, was made Baroness Aldborough and Countess of Walsingham in 1722.
38. She was made Countess of Darlington in 1722.
39. Melville, Lewis (1908). *The First George in Hanover and England: Vol II*. London: Sir Isaac Pitman Random and Sons, Ltd, pp.37–38.

merit her esteem and friendship. I am convinced that she may be advantageously employed in promoting your majesty's [sic] service, and that it will be necessary to employ her; though I will not trust her further than is absolutely necessary."[40]

The reply from the French king was swift and unequivocal. In it is the implicit approval of whatever financial bribes might be necessary to keep this influential woman on side. She had never played politics in Hanover, but this was a different world.

"There is no doubt that the Duchess of Kendal, having a great ascendancy over the King of Great Britain, and maintaining strict union with his ministers, must materially influence their principal resolutions. You will neglect nothing to acquire a share of her confidence, from a conviction that nothing can be more conducive to my interests. There is, however, a manner of giving additional value to the marks of confidence you bestow on her in private, by avoiding in public all appearances which might seem too pointed, by which means you will avoid falling into the inconvenience of being suspected by those who are not friendly to the Duchess, at the same time that a kind of mysteriousness in public on the subject of your confidence, will give rise to a firm belief of your having formed a friendship mutually sincere."[41]

Though she wasn't the monstrous and money-grabbing creature that history has painted her as, it's a certainty that Melusine would have accepted favours or donations from those who sought advancement, just as other influential courtiers had done and would continue to do for centuries. It didn't always work out for them though. Just ask Richard Child, who courted, flattered, and funded Melusine in the hope that he would receive a title for his troubles. His reward was an Irish peerage and the titles of Baron Newtown and Viscount Castlemaine, which both Melusine and Sir Richard took as a thinly veiled insult. They always

---

40. Coxe, William (1798). *Memoirs of the Life and Administration of Robert Walpole, Vol II*. London: T Cadell, Jun, and W Davies, p.301.
41. Melville, Lewis (1908). *The First George in Hanover and England: Vol II*. London: Sir Isaac Pitman Random and Sons, Ltd, pp.38–39.

suspected that Stanhope and his faction had blocked Child's path to a more prestigious English peerage, simply to send a message to the king's mistress. Child had initially hoped to lavish £10,000 on a peerage during Queen Anne's reign, so he certainly wasn't new to such ideas. It had merely taken him longer than expected to act on them.

Still, Melusine had her closed shop from which favours could be purchased, from bestowing a title to granting the relatively lowly wish of 10 year old Horace Walpole to kiss the king's hand, and she no doubt looked favourably upon the gift givers when it came to matters of business. In very few cases did a paper trail remain but once in a while, receipts were left behind. After all, was it really a coincidence that the accounts of the wealthy politician James Brydges showed a payment of £9,500 to Melusine[42] just months before he was awarded the prestigious title of Duke of Chandos? It was an open secret too, and Horace Walpole later noted with sly amusement that when Sir Jacob Bouverie was made Viscount Folkestone, he "bought his ermine at twelve thousand pounds a-yard of the Duchess of Kendal." It was cheap at the price.

Yet there were inevitably some who would be disappointed under the system of courtly favours. Take for instance John Ker of Kersland, who had been a spy in the Hanoverian court for Queen Anne and liked to think that he had played a significant part in securing the succession of King George. Like all loyal servants, he believed that the time had come for him to receive recognition for his service to the Hanoverians. Ker wanted to be made Governor of the Bermudas, but when he received a paltry 100 thalers and a couple of congratulatory medals instead, he became convinced that "one of the foreign concubines" had scuppered his chances. Having missed out on his dream job, Ker's fortunes went from bad to worse and when he ended up in debtor's prison, he attributed his fate entirely to Melusine. Despite his belief, there was nothing to suggest that Ker's suspicions were founded in anything but a very personal hatred for the woman he believed had deliberately set out to ruin him. In the final volume of his memoirs, published by the scandalous Edmund Curll, Ker furiously lamented "the torrent of corruption that inundated the Court when the Hanoverians alighted here, having infested every department of state, from the Lord Chancellor downwards, never has the law been more

---

42. He matched the sum with a similar donation to Sophia Charlotte von Kielmansegg.

distorted in any case to suit political views than it was in that in which this infamous woman was plaintiff." Ker died in debtor's prison in 1726. He blamed Melusine for his sorry fate to his very last breath.

Though Ker's belief that Melusine had set out to ruin him was unfounded, the suggestion that she operated a cash for access and favours scheme was certainly true. In fact, Melusine was unapologetic about it. She had to set herself up for the future and with daughters to support and a lifestyle to finance, she was lining her pockets just like everyone around her. Put simply, titles were certainly up for sale under George I, but they always had been. It was what had oiled the wheels of court since time immemorial.

Popping the Bubble

"*Directors*, for 'tis you I warn,
By long Experience we have found
What Planet rul'd when you were born;
We see you never can be drown'd.

[…]

Oh! May some Western Tempest sweep
These *Locusts* whom our Fruits have fed,
That Plague, *Directors*, to the *deep*,
Driv'n from the *South-Sea* to the *Red*!

[…]

But never shall our isle have Rest,
Till those devouring *Swine* run down,
(The *devils* leaving the *Posses't*)
And headlong in the waters drown.

The Nation then too late will find,
Computing all their Cost and Trouble,
Directors' Promises but Wind,
South-Sea, at best, a mighty BUBBLE."

In verses such as those above, the famed satirist Jonathan Swift devoted page after acerbic page to the evils of the South Sea Bubble, but the warning came too late. When the bubble burst, it was a salutary lesson to Melusine that the life of a royal mistress could be far from a quiet one. The old days in Hanover, where she never meddled in politics and happily played the quiet *hausfrau* for her sullen partner, would soon look more tempting than ever. For now though, with an English peerage under Melusine's belt, all was well once more. She had money, influence, and the title she had craved. Yet all it would take was one disastrous decision to run a coach and horses through her quiet life.

The year 1720 began as it would go on – disastrously. Things got off to a bad start when Melusine's youngest half-brother, Baron Friedrich Wilhelm, died at the age of just 37. Friedrich Wilhelm had gone to bed in perfect health and he had been found dead two hours later, apparently the victim of a stroke. He had been a valued member of the king's household and a close advisor to both George Louis and Melusine, and he was duly honoured with a resting place in the south transept of Westminster Abbey. Melusine sought for something to distract her from her grief and she found it in the act of purchasing an estate in Holstein. Though she would later sell the estate on at a handsome profit, Melusine didn't have time to enjoy building her portfolio before a bout of illness struck her down. She was so sick that it was reported in the press "that her Life was once thought to be in danger"[43], but the episode passed. The Duchess of Kendal recovered her health just in time to enter into one of the most damaging affairs of George Louis' whole reign. The South Sea Bubble was about to inflate.

In between dealing with her own ill health and mourning her beloved brother, Melusine had been forced to watch whilst Walpole and Townshend began to ascend the political ladder once more. Walpole's masterstroke was to encourage the reconciliation of Caroline of Ansbach and George Augustus with the king, and to secure it he had wisely enlisted the help of Melusine. Aware of Caroline's distress at the loss of her children, Walpole suggested that she might find a friend in the king's mistress. A friend who had influence over George I.

Melusine knew that the children would dearly love to see more of their parents, and she went in to bat for the Waleses. The result, in no small part thanks to Walpole and Melusine's intervention, was an uneasy truce between the king and the Prince of Wales. This earned Walpole Caroline of Ansbach's lifelong gratitude and proved once and for all that Melusine could certainly change her partner's mind no matter how intransigent he might initially have seemed. Walpole also used his political influence

---

43. *Original Weekly Journal.* 23 April 1720.

and perhaps a little underhand blackmail to hobble Stanhope and Sunderland, who had bettered him not so long before. With the warring parties forced to shake hands in the Commons just as they had in the royal household, peace was breaking out all over. The only casualty was Walpole's relationship with George Augustus, who regarded him as a schemer. The politician was happy to sacrifice the trust of the prince in exchange for the position of Paymaster of the Forces. He could afford to, after all, for he had Caroline on his side, and would do for as long as she lived.

Regardless of the era, the tempting prospect of getting something for nothing – or very little – has always been difficult to resist. The Georgians were no different in their avarice, and when the South Sea Bubble engulfed the chattering classes with promises of eye-watering wealth and prestige with little to no risk to investors, everyone wanted to be in on it. In the centuries since it almost bankrupted the nation, the story of the South Sea Bubble has become a cautionary tale, a notorious near-legend of a white elephant in which greed and dishonesty combined to create a perfect storm that led people to ruin and, in some cases, an early grave. It also did damage to Melusine's reputation unlike anything she had known before.

The first roots of the bubble were set down in 1711 when a company by the name of *The Governor and Company of the Merchants of Great Britain, trading to the South Seas and other parts of America, and for the encouragement of fishing*, was formed in London. It soon became known by the catchier moniker of *The South Sea Company*, and its fortunes were built on an audacious gamble.

As a new decade approached, the company looked across the Atlantic towards South America, which seemed to promise unbridled wealth. The South Sea Company had been granted a monopoly in 1713 to supply slaves to South America and the company directors envisioned a future in which they could exploit this untapped wealth and take a hefty share of it for themselves. At the time the directors' plans were taking shape, the War of Spanish Succession made efforts to do business in South America an impossibility, but the war wouldn't last forever. The South Sea Company saw an opportunity to be the first through the door when peace broke out. When it applied for and was granted exclusive trading rights to the continent as part of the Peace of Utrecht in 1713, it appeared that the company was well on the way to achieving its goals.

By the time George Louis came to the throne, the South Sea Company was thriving and hugely wealthy. He became its governor in 1718, further cementing its status as one of the central finance institutions of the nation. Buoyed by its impressive new patron, the South Sea Company offered to settle Great Britain's national debt of £30 million, which would offer a much-needed prop to the country's coffers. In return, the nation would pay the company back at a rate of just five per cent interest over a term of twenty-five years.

Such an offer wasn't to be easily dismissed but it didn't come without risks either, although they were small thanks to the government's excellent rate of interest. Besides, the South Sea Company was happy to grease the palms of some influential figures, from politicians to courtiers, to ensure that the risks were downplayed. Sunderland and Stanhope received £100,000 in stocks between them, whilst Postmaster General James Craggs and Chancellor John Aislabie pocketed £30,000 and £20,000 respectively. These politicians in turn made representations to Melusine, the woman who could work an influence on the king that no other could, and the company handed over a cool £15,000 worth of shares to the Duchess of Kendal to ensure that things went their way. As a further sweetener, George Louis and Melusine's youngest daughters were each given £5,000 worth of stock too. With so many senior figures holding so much stock, it was in their best interests that the plan was accepted, for the more money the company made, the more handsome the return shareholders would receive. Melusine would have had no qualms about recommending the scheme to George Louis and it was her advice that he listened to, rather than that of the more pragmatic Robert Walpole. The South Sea Bubble was on its way.

Among the court gossips, there was absolutely no doubt as to why George Louis had championed the scheme so wholeheartedly. As Lady Ormond intimated to Jonathan Swift, he had done as his mistress had told him, whether it was wise to do so or not.

"You remember, and so do I, when the *South-Sea* was said to be my lord *Oxford's* brat, and must be starved at nurse. Now the king has adopted it, and calls it his beloved child; tho', perhaps, you may say, if he loves it no better than his son, it may not be saying much: but he loves it as well as he does the duchess of [Kendal] and that is saying a good deal."[44]

Whatever Walpole and Lady Ormond might think of the idea, people flocked to invest in the South Sea Company and its value went through the roof, increasing by a whopping tenfold. Demand for shares was out of control and everyone wanted a piece of the action, from the wealthiest to the most humble. It was a chance to get rich – or a whole lot richer – very quickly, with a scheme endorsed by the king himself. Who could resist? Not the conmen of Georgian England, that was for sure. As George Louis and Melusine headed off to Hanover, patting themselves on the back for a job well done, the country they left behind exploded with more and more crazy get rich quick schemes. The South Sea Bubble had intoxicated the nation, but it wouldn't stay buoyant for long.

Melusine knew that success in this particular venture might provide her with the nest egg she would surely need should her partner die before her, and she moved fast to ensure the best return on her investment. All too aware of the vagaries of the stock market, she told the chancellor, Aislabie, that he should turn her shares into cash at the earliest and most favourable opportunity. Melusine instructed him "to sell or buy as you would think it the most Profitable and Convenient, for it cannot be pretended that at such a distance as we are [during visits to Hanover] a good and positive Resolution could be taken in the Right time, since those Matters are every moment subject to great alterations."[45] When he failed to do so and the stock began to sink, the usually placid Melusine was furious.

By the autumn of 1720, things had started to go wrong. The company's stock price was plummeting, dropping from nearly £800 to below £150 in the space of a few short weeks. This was caused by the fact, quite simply, that the company had issued more shares than it could ever repay. When word got out that the company directors had sold off their own stocks, people began to panic. In Hanover, George Louis and Melusine were drunk on success and enjoying the high life. By the time the Regency

---

44. Swift, Jonathan (1767). *Letters, Written by Jonathan Swift, DD, and Several of his Friends: Vol II*. London: T Davies, p.157.
45. Georgian Papers Online (http://gpp.rct.uk, November 2020) RA GEO/ MAIN/52844-52845 Letter from the Duchess of Kendal to John Aislabie, 27 September 1720.

Council, which held power in the king's absence, sent word to Germany asking him to return and handle the emerging crisis, it was far too late.

In Hanover, a furious Melusine took up her pen and wrote to Aislabie in the strongest terms, asking why he hadn't disposed of the shares she and her daughters held when the market was at its most healthy. Hoping that there was still time to make a profit, she instructed him that "if the best Occasion [to sell] is miss'd; You will be pleased to make use of those that shall offer themselves for the future, without expecting new advices."[46] The meaning was simple: *get rid of them, because I won't tell you again.*

"If we had been present in England," the Duchess of Kendal continued in one of the few letters of hers that remain, "We would not have fail'd to sell them out, when they were at such an advantageous Price, and I wish you had been so kind as to do it for us, the more when you judged and saw that they was, not to rise, but rather to fall as they have done. I am sorry, our absence made us miss that good Opportunity; and I hope You will be so kind as to take a little care of our Interest, if it is not to[o] great a disadvantage to your other Affairs."[47]

But even as George Louis and Melusine headed for England, Aislabie didn't sell. As the stock value plummeted still further, he feared the consequences for himself and the king should it become public knowledge that he had sold off the shares of the monarch's mistress at a time when the markets were in turmoil. Whatever action Aislabie took, there would be consequences for someone.

The men at the head of the company had no such qualms. They sold off their own stocks just before the crash and in doing so, hastened the company's collapse. When shareholders learned that the men at the very top had bailed out, they scrambled to follow. The more shareholders that sold, the more came forward to follow their example and the once sky-high stock price went into a terminal nosedive. People were ruined, bankrupted, or left suicidal, and in the search for a scapegoat, the ire of the nation turned on the king and his mistress. Supposedly, as Melusine – memorialised by one commentator for "her gigantic skeleton form and Jezebel face" – took the air in her carriage one day in London, a mob gathered to heckle and jeer. When she asked, "Good people, why do

---

46. Ibid.
47. Ibid.

you abuse us? We come for all your goods!", one brave member of the crowed bellowed back, "Aye, and for our chattels too!". It was the South Sea Bubble farrago that led to an accusation that has haunted Melusine ever since, for she and George Louis were already "food for all the venom of the Jacobites," wrote Horace Walpole, "and indeed nothing could be grosser than the ribaldry that was vomited out in lampoons, libels and every channel of abuse, against [George Louis and Melusine], and chanted even in their hearing about the public streets"[48]. Wrong though it was, the belief emerged that the "Five Hundred *Germans* all with empty purses" had sucked the country dry.

In reality, the Hanoverians had done no such thing. What they *had* done was allow their want of money to cloud their good judgment. The country stood on the brink of ruin and revolution, and it was left to Robert Walpole to come to the rescue. Walpole seized control of the nation's perilous finances in the nick of time, keeping it from toppling into total ruin and naturally bolstering his own interests and position as he did so. Besides, he had been smart enough to get out of the South Sea scheme before the crash, pocketing a tidy profit in the process. Cometh the hour, Walpole knew, cometh the man.

As Britain teetered on the edge of bankruptcy and investors counted the catastrophic cost of their losses, one man had much to celebrate. Robert Knight[49], the cashier of the South Sea Company, fled England and made for Calais. He took with him not just a fortune, but was also carrying what was effectively a blackmail list in the form of a ledger containing the names of the very illustrious figures who had been bribed into pushing the company into the ruinous monopoly it had enjoyed. In England, Melusine bore the brunt of the blame for encouraging the king's interests in the company. She had good reason to hope that Knight would never be captured and made to stand trial in England, where he would almost certainly mention her name amongst those who had taken cash for favours. Though Knight had seemingly escaped justice, his colleague John Blunt was less fortunate. Boasting a successful history in the lottery

---

48. Walpole, Horace (1798). *The Works of Horatio Walpole, Earl of Orford: Vol IV.* London: GG and J Robinson, pp.285–286.
49. Knight never returned to England and instead enjoyed a lucrative financial career on the continent. His son, by contrast, had a long and successful parliamentary career, eventually being given the title Earl of Catherlough.

business, Blunt had been made a Baronet in 1720 in recognition of his efforts on behalf of the South Sea Company and had enjoyed a long and lucrative career in the financial markets. The South Sea scheme was his brainchild and when people wanted a scalp, it was his head on the chopping block.

Luckily for Blunt, he just happened to be able to call Robert Walpole an ally and knew that, as long as he did as Walpole asked, he had little to fear. When he was questioned by the newly convened Commons committee into the disaster, Blunt intimated that Melusine was one of the influential patrons who had been happy to receive bribes to further the interests of the company. This was far from ideal, but it was still Knight who had the smoking gun, in the shape of the ledger which listed the bribes and their recipients. Rumour had it that Melusine's name was in that ledger, and the ruthless Knight wouldn't hesitate to drag his champions down with him if he fell. Melusine couldn't afford that book to return to Britain's shores. If it did, the cost to George I and by extension, Melusine, could be catastrophic. They needed Knight to escape at precisely the moment when all of Europe was looking to apprehend him.

It appeared Knight's luck had run out when he was captured in the Brabant by the forces of the Holy Roman Empire, who were prepared to enter talks regarding his extradition to England. No doubt everyone whose name was written in that ledger held their breath, but fortunately for them, the Holy Roman Emperor prevaricated even as British MPs furiously demanded that Knight be returned to face punishment. When they sought George I's intervention he too dragged his heels, assuring parliament that he was doing all he could do secure the extradition of Knight whilst in reality, he was doing as little as possible to achieve it. George Louis pointed out that he had no real legal right to request Knight be expelled from Antwerp and handed over to British custody, all he could do was ask, and hope that the Emperor would comply. Once again, rumour had it that the person behind this heel dragging was Melusine and as a result, she became the subject of a savage satirical print entitled *The Brabant Screen*. In it, the duchess is depicted as a double agent whose identity is protected by a screen from behind which she secretly passes messages to Robert Knight, informing him of the goings on in England and ensuring his continued freedom.

In fact, whilst George Louis was giving the furious politicians his assurances that he would do all he could to see Knight returned to face trial, in private, he was doing quite the opposite. He asked his envoy, William Leathes, to assure his Imperial counterpart, the Marquis de Prié, that should the opportunity arise for Knight to escape, then he shouldn't be prevented from doing so. However, Knight's escape must be achieved "in such a manner that it shall not appear that this escape is authorised by His Majesty or this government."[50]

Unsurprisingly, when the chance came for Knight to escape, he took it. He fled his jailers for a comfortable life in France, where he was to remain for more than two decades. Though the infamous and damning ledger was never recovered, the damage to Melusine and the king had already been done. There might not be any proof of Melusine's involvement in the scam, but her name had been indelibly linked with it. Once more, it was left to Walpole to calm the waters, whilst ensuring that he came out of the whole mess on top.

Walpole wasn't the sort of man to let a chance pass him by. Though some of the guilty were thrown to the wolves and punished for their part in the South Sea Bubble, others were not. Walpole shrewdly made sure that those who could be allies in the future were either censured mildly or not at all. As *Sir Blue String's*[51] reputation as the man who could seemingly achieve the impossible soared, the king's dipped lower and lower. He was jeered at as the dupe who had championed the South Sea Company simply to please his avaricious mistress. In contrast, Walpole's power had never been so great, and he used it to bring down those who had crossed him. He had also finally secured the trust of Melusine, who was immensely grateful to him for rescuing what had seemed like a hopeless situation. Not everyone was so fortunate.

John Aislabie, the Chancellor of the Exchequer who had so annoyed Melusine by failing to sell her shares when the price was at an all-time high and who had managed other royal share portfolios too, was sent to the Tower of London and had to forfeit all the property and cash he

---

50. Pearce, Edward (2011). *The Great Man: Sir Robert Walpole, Scoundrel, Genius and Britain's First Prime Minister*. London: Random House, p.144.
51. The Order of the Knight of the Garter was suspended by a blue ribbon. Since honours could be purchased from Walpole via favours, obedience and influence, after he was awarded the Order of the Garter, he earned himself the nickname *Sir Blue-String*.

had made since 1718. He was later released and lived in comfortable retirement until 1742. Others weren't so lucky: Postmaster General James Craggs the Elder died as a result of a possible suicide in 1721, just one month after the passing of his son, James Craggs the Younger, who had also been implicated in the South Sea Bubble. Just as Aislabie was forced to surrender his funds and property, the estate of Craggs the Elder was forced to relinquish its assets too.

For Lord Stanhope and Lord Sunderland, meanwhile, who had sparred with Walpole and liberally courted the favour of Melusine, the South Sea Bubble was to prove fatal. Sunderland was investigated by the House of Commons but eventually acquitted, although his involvement cost him his political offices. He remained a favourite of George Louis following his resignation but died in 1722 aged just 49.

Stanhope's own fate was no happier. His involvement in the South Sea Company led to an investigation that found he had made no personal profit and showed no dishonesty, but which left an indelible stain on his character. He collapsed during a debate in the House of Lords and perhaps unwisely spent the remainder of the evening at a party thrown by the Duke of Newcastle, where he "drank excessively of new tokay, champagne, visney and barba water, thirteen hours it is said."[52] He died the following day.

For Walpole and his brother-in-law, Viscount Townshend, the South Sea Bubble proved fortuitous. Under Walpole's administration, he enjoyed renewed influence with the king and government alike, some of which he surely owed to Melusine's favour[53]. Little wonder he called her "the good duchess and [our] fast friend". Countess Cowper, Lady of the Bedchamber to the Princess of Wales, wasn't quite so convinced. She dismissed Townshend as "the sneeringest, fawningest Knave that [...] ever strove to put on a Mask, which is no better than an Ass's face"[54]. Countess Cowper, of course, did not hold the reins of government.

52. Pearce, Edward. *The Great Man: Sir Robert Walpole: Scoundrel, Genius and Britain's First Prime Minister* (2011). London: Random House, p.132.
53. When Townshend retired from politics he threw himself wholeheartedly into cultivating the agricultural land at his Raynham Hall home. He had a particular passion for growing turnips and by the time he died was widely known by his nickname of *Turnip Townshend*.
54. Cowper, Mary (1865). *Diary of Mary Countess Cowper, Lady of the Bedchamber to the Princess of Wales, 1714–1720*. London: John Murray, p.114.

Ass or not, Walpole and Townshend now commanded the affairs of state more thoroughly than ever before. Count de Broglio, the French envoy to Britain, knew this without a doubt when he wrote to inform his employer that, "[Lord Townshend and Mr. Walpole] should remain in power, for they appear anxious to maintain the good intelligence which subsists between the two crowns; they possess an unbounded influence over the king and the duchess of Kendal, they enjoy the whole power of government, and the entire confidence of the king."[55]

Robert Walpole received a rather loftier epithet. To this day, he is recognised as the first Prime Minister of Great Britain.

---

55. Coxe, William (1798). *Memoirs of the Life and Administration of Robert Walpole, Vol II.* London: T Cadell, Jun, and W Davies, p.301.

Making Coin

Though Robert Walpole emerged from the crisis of the South Sea Bubble more powerful than ever, Melusine had been badly stung. Rare indeed were the occasions on which she stuck her head above the parapet, and during the South Sea Bubble fiasco, it had nearly been taken off. It would have been wise for her to retire to the background for a while and let the dust settle, but the whole affair had ruffled her usually settled feathers. To add insult to injury she had made far less profit than she had hoped, and certainly not enough to set her up for life. Melusine had always been aware that her position, though secure whilst George Louis lived, might become precarious if he predeceased her. George Louis did what he could to ensure she would be taken care of, but the more money she had, the more it seemed that she needed just to keep her household afloat. After all, when the newspapers reported that "the Dutchess [sic] of Kendal has five thousand Pounds worth of Jewels fix'd on her Birth Day cloaths,"[56] it was hardly surprising that people began to wonder where the money was coming from. Those who feared that the Hanoverians were set on leeching England dry were just waiting to point the finger.

Though George Louis had hoped that he would be able to add Melusine to the Civil List, he had learned early on that this wish wasn't going to be granted. This meant that he had to finance her via other means, which led partly to Melusine's reputation for avarice. She certainly lived well, but she was unfailingly generous with her family and dependents, including rustling up the cash to bail out her brother, Daniel Bodo, whose ruinously expensive love of alchemy threatened to bankrupt the family estates. Such gestures were second nature to Melusine, who never forgot how her family had rallied together on the death of their mother, or how they had claimed hers and George Louis' illegitimate children as their own without a second thought. In stark contrast to the often poisonous

---

56. *Original Weekly Journal.* 28 May 1720.

relations between the Hanoverian royals, the von der Schulenberg children remained as close as ever.

Leafing through the newspapers of the 1720s, one can easily find frequent reports of Melusine's philanthropy, from restoring churches to making large charitable donations. She even settled the accounts of debtors, as was the occasional wont of the rich who were keen to secure their reward in heaven. Melusine was an extravagant churchgoer, and could be glimpsed attending Lutheran services seven times each Sunday, much to the amusement of her detractors. When the minister of the chapel in the Savoy refused her permission to enter due to her position as a mistress, she merely took her pious business to a church that would be more welcoming. The minister was soon replaced by a more compliant candidate.

On top of the income from her property in Holstein, Melusine received a pension of £7,500 from George Louis, but it still wasn't enough to meet the needs of the king's favourite mistress. To assuage her concerns, in 1722 George Louis arranged for Melusine to receive the patent for the Irish coinage from the Earl of Sunderland. This essentially gave Melusine the legal right to produce Ireland's copper coinage, but she had no interest whatsoever in the business of manufacture. When Melusine received the patent, she saw an opportunity to make a killing and swiftly disposed of it at a handsome profit.

Melusine sold the patent to an ironmaster named William Wood for the enormous sum of £10,000. Wood had previously minted coins known as the *Rosa Americana* for circulation in North America, so this was far from new ground for him. The Irish patent authorised its holder to produce 360 tons of halfpennies and farthings for fourteen years. Wood would earn 30p in each pound and was required to pay an annual fee of £800 to the king until the patent expired. He set to work minting the coins in Phoenix Street, Seven Dials, but there was trouble from the outset. The patent allowed that the coins could be turned away by merchants in Ireland should they wish and for those who were doing the maths regarding the cost to purchase the patent and the annual fee to keep hold of it, there seemed to be only one way that Wood could profit from the deal. He would either have to commit fraud or debase the coins, minting them from the basest metals possible and effectively producing money that was worth less in metal than its face value. Rumour had it that once

Wood's coinage began to turn a profit, he had an arrangement to split the dividend with the Duchess of Kendal. The rumour was unfounded.

The people of Ireland were understandably furious that their coinage had been handed first to a king's mistress, then sold off to a man who seemed to have little ambition beyond profit. Their cause was taken up by Jonathan Swift, who wrote:

> "When late a feminine magician,
> Join'd with a brazen politician,
> Expos'd to blind a nation's eyes,
> A parchment of prodigious size;
> Conceal'd behind that ample screen,
> There was no silver to be seen.
> But to this parchment let the Drapier
> Oppose his countercharm of paper,
> And ring Wood's copper in our ears
> So loud till all the nation hears;
> That sound will make the parchment shrivel,
> And drive the conjurers to the Devil:
> And when the sky is grown serene,
> Our silver will appear again."

Though Swift refrained from naming names it was obvious that Melusine was the *feminine magician* and the politician, we might reasonably suspect, was the all-powerful Robert Walpole. Playing with court favours was one thing but playing with a kingdom's currency was another. At first dissent was muted but it grew louder and more vociferous until the Irish Parliament officially lodged a protest with George Louis in September 1723. They argued that there was no shortage of copper coinage in Ireland, so Wood's new allocation arriving in bulk would cause a leap in inflation and may even lead to gold and silver becoming scarce. As the land would be flooded with new base coins, those containing valuable precious metals might be taken out of circulation since their gold and silver content would be worth more if it was melted down. Wood's coins were easy to forge due to their quality, so the official allocation might be the tip of the iceberg. Ireland could be overwhelmed.

Swift wrote a series of anonymous pamphlets on the subject known as *The Drapier's Letters*, in which he set out the complaints of the Irish people and policymakers. At their heart was the argument that Ireland's currency had been used as a plaything for Melusine, nothing more than an easy way for a mistress to make money. In an effort to allay the fears of the Irish people and silence Melusine's critics, the then Master of the Mint, celebrated physicist Sir Isaac Newton, agreed to perform tests on Wood's coins to ascertain whether they were indeed debased. Newton was assisted by Edward Southwell, Secretary of the Privy Council of Ireland, and John Scrope, Treasury Secretary. Their report concluded that:

> "[The] copper of which Mr Wood's coinage is made is of the same goodness and value with the copper of which the copper money is coined in your Majesty's mint for England.
>
> [...]
>
> It likewise appears, that the halfpence and farthings coined by Mr Wood, when compared to the copper money coined for Ireland in the reigns of King Charles II. King James II. and King William and Queen Mary, considerably exceeds them all in weight, very far exceeds them in all goodness, firmness and value of the copper."[57]

Yet Swift and his fellow critics were not at all convinced by the external panel's findings. They were quick to point out that the coins Newton and his peers were given to test had been provided by Wood himself and asked how it was that Wood hoped to turn a profit if all the coins he minted conformed to the high standards that Newton had confirmed. They had no doubt that Newton's experiments and conclusions were honest, based on the coins that had been submitted for testing, but they refused to believe that Wood was equally above board.

Walpole had been wary of the plan for the Irish coinage from the off. Not, as his Victorian biographer claimed, because "an irritable and discontented race like the Irish would object to any improvement in their

---

57. Scott, Walter (ed.) (1814). *The Works of Jonathan Swift: Vol VII*. Edinburgh: Archibald Constable and Co, pp.128–129.

currency, unless everything connected with the scheme was exclusively Irish — the contractor to be an Irishman, the copper to be Irish metal, and the coin to be turned out from a mint in Dublin,"[58] but because he knew it was bound to become a flashpoint for yet more dissent. Once Swift took up the cause though, the matter of Irish coinage exploded into the popular consciousness and its critics grew louder than ever.

Walpole had no doubt where the attacks and rumours had originated, and he pointed the finger at his political rival Lord Carteret. Carteret had the ear of the king and unlike Walpole, was fluent in German. He was also a personal favourite of Jonathan Swift, whose *Drapier's Letters* had been such a prolonged and savage attack on the affair of Wood's coinage, and Walpole had long since distrusted him. When Melusine's favourite, Lord Sunderland, died in 1722, Carteret had written to the king to warn him that he was surrounded by enemies in the guise of friends and, naturally, to seek his own advancement. It was Melusine who tried to calm Carteret's fears and "bid him have patience, and told him the king hated his other ministers"[59]. Instead Carteret persevered in his push for promotion, allying himself to Melusine's lifelong rival, Madame von Kielmansegg. He attempted to win her favour by procuring a promotion at the French court for her daughter's fiancé, an endeavour which proved to be ill-judged. As we shall learn elsewhere in this volume, Carteret's efforts were frustrated by Melusine's political allies and the massed senior courtiers of Versailles. It was hardly surprising that there was animosity between Melusine and Walpole on one side, and Carteret on the other.

It was this animosity, Walpole was sure, that gave Carteret a motive for clandestinely whipping up untruths and anger over the coinage. In fact, Walpole had little interest in the Irish patent other than to keep Melusine on his side and when the scandal exploded, it dragged him in. He wrote to Townshend to complain that "[Carteret] flings dirt upon me, who passed the patent, and makes somebody [the Duchess of Kendal] uneasy, for whose sake it was done; and this is one of the instances wherein those that think themselves in danger begin to be upon the offensive."[60]

58. Ewald, Charles Alex (1878). *Sir Robert Walpole: A Political Biography*. London: Chapman and Hall, p.174.
59. Ballantyne, Archibald (1887). *Lord Carteret: A Political Biography*. London: Richard Bentley & Son, p.82.
60. Ibid., pp.111–112.

Yet all of Walpole's suspicions were based on nothing but circumstantial evidence. Carteret had allied himself with Kielmansegg over Schulenberg and had influential Whig friends in Ireland, as well as a close personal friendship with Jonathan Swift, but whilst there is nothing concrete to suggest that he might have whipped up a whispering campaign, it's certainly very possible. The Irish coinage scandal exploded into a wider debate about the right of Ireland to govern itself, leading to calls for an Ireland that was independent of the English Parliament, but still governed by King George I. Soon Walpole was fighting a battle that he had little anticipated and was left with no choice but to climb down. The patent was withdrawn and Walpole, who had supported it in public, was left embarrassed.

In the wake of the coinage controversy, Walpole's opponent Lord Carteret was dispatched to Ireland to replace the Duke of Grafton as Lord Lieutenant. Though intended as a sideways move, this was to prove fortuitous for his career. If Walpole hoped the new office in Ireland would be his rival's undoing, he was to be frustrated. Instead Carteret proved to be a popular figure with the Irish. He calmed the lingering unrest and remained in office for six years. There was compensation for Wood too. Though he lost his patent, he was mollified with a compensatory pension of £3000 per year for the next eight years[61].

Swift, meanwhile, turned his nib on the king's household once more in his anonymous work, *A Wicked Treasonable Libel*, a manuscript of which was found amongst Swift's papers, written in his own handwriting. On the back he had noted, "A traitorous Libel, writ several [sic] Years ago. [...] Copyed [sic] Septr 9th 1735. I wish I knew the Author, that I might hang him." Swift's disclaimer rather cleverly pointed the finger of blame for the authorship of the poem at someone else, but there was no such concession to decency in the text itself. Melusine might not have been named, but it was obvious who the piece was about – and it was obvious too who had written it.

> "While the King and his ministers keep up such a pother,
> And all about changing one whore for another,
> Think I to myself what need all this strife,

---

61. He died in 1730.

His majesty [sic] first had a whore of a wife,
And surely the difference mounts to no more
Than, now he has gotten a wife of a whore."

The affair of the Irish coinage left Melusine embarrassed and Walpole rattled. Popular opinion blamed her avarice for the mess and for the upheaval it had caused both in Ireland and at Westminster. The whole debacle had shone a spotlight on concerns that Ireland felt had been allowed to fester for too long, and the debate over the autonomy of the Irish Parliament and people over their own nation. For a woman who had done her best to avoid involvement in political rows, things couldn't really have been much worse. Yet Melusine wasn't cowed. With her political dabblings silenced for now, she turned her attention to matters matrimonial.

Wedding Plans

When George I came to England, he commanded his son to join him. George Augustus, the new Prince of Wales, obeyed with little enthusiasm. With neither the elector nor his heir left in Hanover, George Louis decided that his grandson, Frederick, would stay in the ancestral electorate and act as an official figurehead. At the time of George Louis and George Augustus' departure, Fred was only seven and, just as the relationship between the king and his son had grown increasingly frosty, now the relationship between George Augustus and his own heir would follow the same sorry path. George Augustus and Caroline of Ansbach were forbidden by the king from returning to Hanover at all and instead, George Louis became young Fred's mentor and guide. As the bond between grandfather and grandson deepened, George Augustus became more and more convinced that his father was poisoning his son against him, leading to yet another fracture in the House of Hanover.

As the years went on and his grandchildren grew, George Louis began to comb the courts of Europe for suitable spouses for them. He found some likely candidates in the Prussian court of his daughter, Sophia Dorothea of Hanover, and her husband, Frederick William I. Marriage between the couple's children and those of George Augustus seemed like an elegant solution to the problem of finding suitable spouses. The Houses of Hanover and Hohenzollern would be more powerful than ever if the cousins were to marry, furthering the dynastic ambitions of George Louis and Frederick William alike. Crucially, just as the doomed marriage between George Louis and Sophia Dorothea had been conceived to ensure that money and territory stayed in the family, marriages between the courts of Great Britain and Prussia would serve the same end.

George Louis and Melusine took a trip to the continent and visited the Hohenzollern court to discuss the possibility of a double wedding. The proposed marriages would unite George Augustus' second daughter, Amelia, and eldest son, Frederick, with their cousins, the future Frederick the Great and Wilhelmine of Prussia. The marriage plans had originally been mooted by George Louis' late mother, the formidable Electress Sophia, and they had been enthusiastically rekindled by George Louis' daughter, Sophia Dorothea of Hanover. It was Sophia Dorothea who kept her father's interest in the scheme alive, but she'd reckoned without a vengeful governess looking to make trouble.

Wilhelmine was cared for in her youth by a governess named Léti, who was the daughter of a monk. Léti had been recommended to the family by Melusine's rival, Sophia Charlotte von Kielmansegg, and it was through her that Sophia Charlotte was kept abreast of everything that was happening in the Prussian court. Léti was a brutal caretaker who regularly beat her charge black and blue, but Wilhelmine was too frightened of her retaliation to tell her parents what was happening. With nobody to challenge her, Léti's tyranny continued and she punctuated her cruelties with everything from gentleman callers to court intrigues, as her abuse went unnoticed. Eventually Léti decided that she deserved more than the simple privileges of a governess and she enlisted her old friend, Sophia Charlotte, by now Countess of Darlington, to help her get what she believed was her due. Sophia Charlotte wrote a letter in which she promised Léti a role at the British court if she was willing to leave Prussia. Léti showed it to Queen Sophia Dorothea, expecting that her mistress would offer all manner of sweeteners to keep her from accepting Lady Darlington's generous offer. Needless to say, things didn't quite go to plan.

Sophia Dorothea was aware of the influence of Sophia Charlotte over the king and feared that Léti could cause all sorts of trouble in George Louis' household. When the conflicted queen didn't immediately meet Léti's demands she tightened the screws, but the added pressure backfired on her. Léti had gone too far and this time, Wilhelmine's maids spoke up. They told Wilhelmine's horrified parents all about the beatings, which left Frederick William beside himself with anger. It was only Sophia Dorothea's surprisingly merciful intervention that stopped the furious king from having the brutal governess incarcerated and instead he contented himself with exiling Léti from court. She remained as shameless as ever and when she left, she took with her a closet full of Wilhelmine's finest gowns and all the gifts she had received throughout her employment. Her haul was worth a small fortune.

Léti headed for England and the household of Sophia Charlotte, Countess of Darlington, where she conceived a spiteful plan to ruin Wilhelmine's marriage prospects. She plied Sophia Charlotte with fictitious but shocking accounts of Wilhelmine's bad character, claiming that the young lady was violently insane. Years later Wilhelmine discovered that Léti had claimed her temper was "as bad as I was ugly, and [so] violent that my violence often caused me to have epileptic fits."[62]

Dripping in false sincerity and perfectly pitched concern, Sophia Charlotte helpfully conveyed Léti's reports to George Louis, aware that she would be scuppering the marriage plans in doing so. With the king and his mistress about to travel to Hanover and ink the contract on the prospective double marriage, her timing couldn't have been better.

When Sophia Dorothea and Frederick William met George Louis in Hanover, they were expecting that signing off the double marriage would be a matter of formality. Instead they found George Louis happy to agree to the marriage of Amelia and Frederick, but considerably less enthusiastic about the proposed match between Fred and Wilhelmine. Sophia Dorothea was furious. She had nurtured plans for the double wedding for years and spent a considerable amount of money in doing so. To have it undermined by a mere servant was an insult. Caught in the middle of a power play between the Countess of Darlington and the Duchess of Kendal, she was determined not to let her plans fall victim to Léti and Sophia Charlotte's scheming.

Sophia Dorothea knew better than to argue the point with her father and instead took the well-trodden path to Melusine's door, no doubt with her purse strings suitably loosened. Soon the Duchess of Kendal was encouraging George Louis to approve the marriage of Fred and Wilhelmine and eventually he agreed to visit Berlin and meet his granddaughter in person. Only then could he really know if Léti and Sophia Charlotte's damning reports of the girl were true.

On the night of the king's arrival in Berlin, Sophia Dorothea prepared her daughter to meet him with a sergeant major's eye for detail. Wilhelmine wasn't a slender girl but Sophia Dorothea laced her so tight that she could neither eat nor drink and when Wilhelmine dared to voice doubts about

---

62. Christian of Schleswig Holstein (1887). *Memoirs of Wilhelmine, Margravine of Baireuth*. New York: Scribner & Welford, p.43.

marrying a suitor she didn't know, her mother went into a rage that would have shamed even Léti. Sophia Dorothea picked up where Léti had left off, constantly criticising Wilhelmine for her behaviour or language, telling her that Fred wouldn't approve of this or that and reminding her that this was all for her own good. Yet if she had to change to please her bridegroom, Wilhelmine decided that she would rather remain unmarried. "I went in despair to my own room," she admitted after she was dismissed from her mother's company after yet another showdown, "determined that my consent should not be so easily gained."[63]

When George Louis and Melusine arrived in Berlin, Wilhelmine and her brother Frederick were presented to the royal party. George Louis took a candle and silently passed it over Wilhelmine, examining her from head to toe with an expression of utter disdain. Without saying a word, he put the candle down and turned to address Frederick, at which point George Louis suddenly transformed into the very model of an avuncular grandfather. He was as chatty and good humoured with the young man as he had been sullen and imperious to his sister. For Wilhelmine, it was an upsetting experience and one that shines a harsh light on the lot of a young female royal.

The whole trip was planned with military precision and the sole aim of securing the two marriages, but when George Louis fell ill those plans were thrown into disarray. The king had just finished dining when he collapsed to the ground in a dead faint. When he regained consciousness he could barely speak and had to be helped to bed. It's likely that George Louis had suffered a mini-stroke and though he made a swift recovery, Melusine was shaken by the stark reminder that he was getting older and more infirm with every passing day. Yet George Louis was soon back on his feet and at the end of the festivities, the matter was decided. The hard sell had paid off and there would be a double marriage between the grandchildren of King George I. When it came to the battle of Sophia Charlotte and Melusine, it looked as though Melusine had got her way. In fact, her victory was a fleeting one.

In the end neither of the marriages took place. The death of King George I put a stop to the plans for a double marriage once and for all, as his successor sought to stamp his own mark on the court he had inherited

---

63. Ibid., p.45.

and called off negotiations[64]. By that point, the ambitious Countess of Darlington was long dead and for the grieving Melusine, dynastic marriages were of no interest whatsoever. For now, though, the victory was hers to enjoy.

---

64. Wilhelmine eventually married Frederick, Margrave of Brandenburg-Bayreuth, in 1731. Frederick had been betrothed to Wilhelmine's sister but her father decided that Wilhelmine would be the better candidate, despite not involving the groom-to-be in his decision. Wilhelmine resisted the marriage at first but eventually capitulated and though the couple were initially happy, they became estranged when Frederick took a mistress.

Bolingbroke

Despite her apparent triumph in Berlin, Melusine was still smarting from the stinging aftermath of the South Sea Bubble and the Irish coinage scandal. She was depicted in print and caricature as the sort of woman who would ransom off a kingdom's coin for her own financial benefit, and whose avaricious desperation to acquire ever more cash had almost led the nation into catastrophe. Though Robert Walpole won Melusine's gratitude and favour after he steered the country out of what had seemed like inevitable ruin, she never picked up any of his political nous. Walpole knew when and how to keep out of trouble and that was a lesson that Melusine would have done well to learn. After her decades of uneventful companionship in Hanover, the Duchess of Kendal was simply no match for the twists and turns of British politics, no matter how grand her title.

Henry St John, 1st Viscount Bolingbroke, had once flown high. He had been the leader of the Tories, and he had held one senior cabinet post after another during the reign of Queen Anne, but when George I came to the throne all of that changed. Lord Bolingbroke had been a firm supporter of Queen Anne and when discussions were taking place regarding the Hanoverian claims to the throne during the late queen's lifetime, he always tended to look more favourably on Anne's interests than those of her eventual successors. It was to prove a costly mistake in the long term for when George I arrived in England, one of his first acts was to dismiss Bolingbroke.

Lord Bolingbroke's subsequent actions were difficult to explain. Having failed to protect his position and that of the Tories, he fled the country "in Disguise, having a black bob Wig on, with a laced Hat, and very ordinary Clothes"[65], and made for France. There he allied himself to James Francis Edward Stuart, the Jacobite Pretender, who he believed had a more valid claim to the British throne than the Hanoverians. In France,

---

65. *London Gazette.* 29 March 1715–2 April 1715; issue 5316.

Bolingbroke served as foreign minister for the Jacobites, but he soon came to realise that he had made a fatal error in leaving his homeland. Though the Pretender made him the Earl of Bolingbroke in the Jacobite peerage, in England, Lord Bolingbroke was attainted for treason in his absence and stripped of all his titles and property. To all intents and purposes, he had been cut adrift. Only then did he realise that he didn't want to be in France at all.

From his exile in France, Bolingbroke looked back at Britain longingly. He wanted to come home, but with his old sparring partner Robert Walpole holding almost unchallenged power, the question was how could he do so? When a letter-writing campaign brought no joy, he knew that he would have to appeal to the heart of the royal bosom itself. Just as other courtiers had done before him, Bolingbroke turned to Melusine as his key to winning the favour of the king.

Not long after the death of Bolingbroke's first, ill-treated wife[66], Frances Winchcombe, he married again. His new spouse was a French widow named Marie Claire Deschamps de Marcilly, whose late husband had been the Marquis de Villette, cousin of Louis XIV's morganatic[67] wife, Mme de Maintenon. The second Mrs Bolingbroke was wealthy and well-connected, and she agreed to go to England and court Melusine, armed with a bribe of £11,000. No doubt Melusine, who "hath been slightly indisposed for some days past [...] with the Colick"[68], was glad of a new income stream as she convalesced.

Walpole was minded not to allow Bolingbrook to return from exile, but he had no power to block Bolingbroke's return to favour if it was what George Louis wanted. Once the door to Melusine's chambers closed, the monarch's ear was hers alone. When Marie Claire arrived at the British court she set about immediately endearing herself to Melusine, who had learned from the South Sea Bubble and William Wood debacles not to leave a paper trail that could lead critics back to her door. This time the money that bought her favours was not passed directly to the Duchess

---

66. Bolingbroke was known for his wild living and orgiastic tendencies. Marriage did nothing to soften them.

67. A morganatic marriage is one in which one spouse is of a significantly lower rank than the other. That spouse is denied the right to inherit privileges and rank should their partner die.

68. *Post Boy.* 12 January 1723–15 January 1723; issue 5224.

of Kendal, but to Viscount Chetwynd. The viscount handed it to the Countess of Walsingham, Melusine's daughter, and from her it found its way to Melusine, "whom English money and an English Title had made true to the English ministers"[69].

Walpole's chaplain, Henry Etough, recalled that:

> "[Walpole] informed me the same day, that the bill in favour of St. John, is wholly to be ascribed to the influence of the Dutchess. Either the present viscount Chetwin [sic], or his brother William, conveyed eleven thousand pounds from St. John's lady to lady Walsingham, the dutchess' niece."[70]

Though in these times of cash-for-access scandals it may appear surprising that such a bribe took place, the exchange of court favours wasn't uncommon. There was also the small matter of Marie Claire's considerable wealth, which certainly opened doors in the Georgian world. She swiftly became Melusine's shadow, making her husband's case at every opportunity, whilst Bolingbroke waited for updates in France. The first victory came with his pardon in May 1723, though his titles and lands remained forfeit. Welcomed back into the fold, Bolingbroke planned to ingratiate himself with the king during the monarch's latest European jaunt, then accompany him back to Great Britain once his business in Hanover was concluded.

> "An Express is dispatch'd to the Lord Viscount Bolingbroke, with an Account of his Pardon pass'd and as his Lordship will wait his Majesty's arrival in Holland, so we are well assured that his Lordship will follow the Court to Hanover."[71]

A thrilled and no doubt relieved Bolingbroke wrote to Lord Townshend in full forelock-tugging mode to tell him:

---

69. Cowper, Mary (1865). *Diary of Mary Countess Cowper, Lady of the Bedchamber to the Princess of Wales, 1714-1720.* London: John Murray, p.145.
70. Coxe, William (1798). *Memoirs of the Life and Administration of Robert Walpole: Vol II.* London: T Cadell, Jun, and W Davies, p.345.
71. *Daily Journal.* 31 May 1723; issue 735.

"I shall do my best on this side of the water to lessen the force of any objections against what the king has done, and intends to do in my favour; and if my restitution can be compleated [sic], your lordship may have more useful friends and servants; a more faithful one you cannot have, than I shall endeavour to approve myself. Mr Walpole tells me, that I may give your lordship the trouble of delivering the two inclosed [sic], which I beg of you to present to the king, and to the dutchess [sic] of Kendal."[72]

Melusine replied via Townshend to assure Bolingbroke of his allies' "good intentions to have what remains to be done in your favour perfectly finished according to your desire"[73]. The letter stopped short of issuing a guarantee and reminded the ever-hopeful Bolingbroke "that it does not entirely depend on the king; and that it must be managed with circumspection."[74] In the same letter Townshend assured Bolingbroke that he was "desired by the dutchess [sic] of Kendall [sic], to return your lordship very many thanks for your letter to her, with assurances of her grace's particular regard for your lordship and the success of your affairs."[75] Winning Melusine to his cause would prove to be an intelligent move.

Townshend's letter confirmed that Marie Claire had done her job admirably, or most of it anyway. What Bolingbroke wanted next was the reinstatement of his titles, lands, and a seat in the House of Lords. When he fell dangerously ill with a fever in late 1724 it seemed as though he might never live to see his triumph[76], but once again fate smiled on the seemingly charmed Bolingbroke and he pulled through. He arrived back in England in late May 1725 to be greeted by reports that the attainder would soon be lifted. This meant that his titles and estates would be restored and would be able to pass down the line of succession to his son. Finally, on the last day of May, George Louis attended the House of Lords and gave the royal Assent to "An Act for enabling Henry St. John, late

72. Coxe, William (1798). *Memoirs of the Life and Administration of Robert Walpole: Vol II.* London: T Cadell, Jun, and W Davies, p.311.
73. Ibid.
74. Ibid., p.312.
75. Ibid.
76. No sooner did Bolingbroke recover than his wife fell dangerously ill. She too recovered and lived until 1750. Her husband died the following year.

1. Ehrengard Melusina von der Schulenberg, Duchess of Kendal.

2. Mrs Howard, Countess of Suffolk, after Charles Jervas.

3. Lady Henrietta Howard, after Thomas Gibson, 1720.

Georgius D:G: Mag: Brit: Fran: et Hib: Rex: F: D:
Brun: et Lunen: Dux: R: I: Arch: Thesaur: et Princeps Elector &c:
Inauguratus 20 die Octobris 1714

4. King George I, John Faber, after D Stevens, 1722.

5. George Augustus, Prince of Wales, later George II, by Sir Godfrey Kneller, 1724.

6. Sophia Dorothea of Celle, wife of George I.

7. Caroline of Ansbach, wife of George II, by Alexander van Haecken, after Jacopo Amigoni, 1736.

8. Electress Sophia, mother of George I, by Petrus Schenck.

9. Countess Clara von Platen.

CLARA ELIESABETA
VERMÆHLETE
GRÆFFIN VON PLATEN
GEBOHRNE VON MEYSENBUGH.

10. Count Philip Christoph von Königsmarck, lover of Sophia Dorothea of Celle.

11. The murder of Count von Königsmarck.

12. Sophia Charlotte von Kielmansegg, Countess of Darlington, half-sister and falsely rumoured to be the mistress of George I, after Sir Godfrey Kneller.

13. George II Augustus, by Alexander van Haecken, after Sandie, 1736.

14. *Tea Party at Lord Harrington's House, St. James's*, by Charles Philips, 1730. George Berkeley leans on the left of the mantelpiece, with Henrietta Howard seated beside him to his right.

15. Horace Walpole, by Henry Hoppner Meyer, after Sir Thomas Lawrence, 1795.

Peint par Richardson

Gravé par Ambroise Tardieu

WILLIAM CHESELDEN.

16. William Cheselden, by Jonathan Richardson.

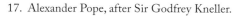
17. Alexander Pope, after Sir Godfrey Kneller.

18. Lord John Hervey.

19. Mary Lepell, Lady Hervey, by James Heath, 1798.

20. Robert Walpole, by Jacob Houbraken, after Arthur Pond, 1746.

21. Jonathan Swift, by Pierre Fourdrinier, after Charles Jervas.

Swift triumphs here lett pining envy know it
the fairest nymph protects the brightest Poet
Her Tast correct no other pen can hitt
no other smiles so well reward his witt

22. John Gay, after Sir Godfrey Kneller.

23. Baroness von Kielmansegg, Countess of Darlington, after Sir Godfrey Kneller.

24. Philip Dormer Stanhope, 4th Earl of Chesterfield, son-in-law of Melusine von der Schulenberg, after William Hoare.

25. *The South Sea Scheme*, by William Hogarth, 1721.

26. *Robin's Reign*, mocking corruption in the government of Robert Walpole, by Caleb D'Anvers, 1731.

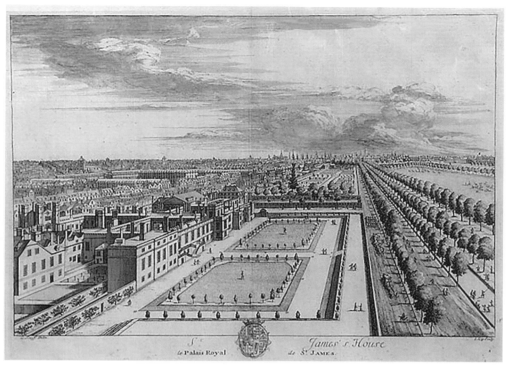

27. St James's Palace and the Mall.

28. Kensington Palace, photographed by George Tsiagalakis.

29. Leicester House, 1748.

30. Marble Hill House, North Side, photographed by Jim Linwood.

Viscount Bolingbroke, and the Heirs Male of his Body, notwithstanding his Attainder, to take and enjoy several Manors, Lands and Hereditaments in the Counties of Wilts, Surrey and Middlesex"[77]. In short, Bolingbroke was back in the game. That payment of £11,000 to Melusine wouldn't have done his case any harm whatsoever.

Although "Viscount *Bolingbroke* kiss'd the King's Hand and continued some Time with his [sic] Majesty,"[78] there were caveats. He had little real political influence and he was denied the right to sell or transfer the ownership of any of his property. Likewise, whilst Walpole might not have been able to block Bolingbroke from being pardoned, he did manage to prevent the return of his title and seat in the House of Lords. Perhaps surprisingly, Bolingbroke was so filled with his own self-importance that he honestly believed that the king would throw Walpole out of office and hand him the reins of power. Even more surprisingly, if Walpole's chaplain Henry Etough is to be believed, Walpole was anticipating the same outcome. And he believed it was all down to the influence of Melusine von der Schulenberg. Etough recalled Walpole's fears that, "As [Bolingbroke] had the dutchess [sic] entirely on his side, I need not add, what must or might in time have been the consequence."[79]

Walpole's fears and Bolingbroke's hopes would prove to be misplaced. George Louis might have restored Bolingbroke to favour, but the possibility of him replacing Walpole with Bolingbroke was always remote. Still, it does tell us something of Melusine's influence that even Walpole feared for his position once Bolingbroke had purchased her favour. The once-disgraced Bolingbroke was even granted a private audience with George Louis at Melusine's request, though the king cleared the plan with Walpole first. It sent the politician into an uncharacteristic panic.

Walpole knew that he was in an impossible position. Should he tell George Louis not to meet with Bolingbroke then Melusine would simply press harder to get her way. Should he approve the meeting, then Bolingbroke would doubtless use the private audience to stick the knife into his opponent. An unsealed letter from Bolingbroke to the king that happened to pass over Walpole's desk left him certain that his old rival

---

77. *London Gazette*. 29 May 1725–1 June 1725; issue 6377.
78. *British Journal*. 5 June 1725; issue 142.
79. Coxe, William (1798). *Memoirs of the Life and Administration of Robert Walpole: Vol II*. London: T Cadell, Jun, and W Davies, p.345.

was intending to oust him, but Walpole told George Louis to meet with Bolingbroke anyway, determined to carry out some damage limitation immediately afterwards.

As the monarch and the once-exiled politician met in private, Walpole fretted and paced in an antechamber immediately outside. When the meeting ended and Walpole was admitted to the sovereign's company, he asked the king what had been discussed. George Louis' worryingly vague reply was simply, "bagatelles, bagatelles", but Walpole was sure that his old foe was elbowing his way back into power. With Melusine as his champion, he feared where it might end. A confident Bolingbroke, meanwhile, readied himself for power.

In 1726 Bolingbroke and George Louis' relationship was closer than ever and Bolingbroke was convinced that he would soon be installed in Robert Walpole's place at the head of government. Once the king returned from a trip to Hanover, Bolingbroke assured his supporters that there would be a handover of power and Walpole's reign would be over. Thanks to George Louis' death during his last visit to his ancestral electorate, that moment never came. Instead fate took a decisive swerve and Bolingbroke's "fortune turned rotten at the very moment it grew ripe"[80], sending his ambitions into oblivion along with the late king.

Yet Bolingbroke continued to build his influence and massage Melusine's ego for what remained of George Louis' life. He hoped that Melusine would pave his way to the very top of the administration and Walpole certainly believed that she had the ability and inclination to do so. In fact, though Melusine's influence held considerable sway, whether it reached far enough to unseat Robert Walpole is a matter for debate. It's equally unlikely that George Louis would have agreed to such a radical change of command just to satisfy Melusine's whims. Walpole was a fixer, and a fixer was just what the king wanted at the top of the political tree. The South Sea Bubble had left him burned. He and Melusine alike knew better than anyone that the intervention of Robert Walpole had been all that had prevented a complete incineration.

---

80. Swift, Jonathan (1767). *Letters, Written by Jonathan Swift, DD, and Several of his Friends: Vol II*. London: T Davies, p.257.

A Left-Handed Marriage

"It is reported, That her Grace the Dutchess [sic] of *Kendal* is honour'd by his Imperial Majesty with the Dignity of the Princess of the Empire."[81]

With the Irish coinage debacle laid to rest and the memory of the South Sea Bubble slowly fading, Melusine was once again comfortable. When the Holy Roman Emperor Charles VI made her a princess of the Holy Roman Empire in 1723, it was a mark not only of her prestige, but also her loyalty. She was even a correspondent of the empress herself, a sure sign of Melusine's acceptance amongst the courts of Europe. Whilst Sophia Dorothea continued in her genteel confinement in Celle it was George Louis' mistress who was to all intents and purposes his queen. It was the newly-minted Princess of Eberstein who travelled at his side, who had his ear and who "gave a magnificent Entertainment to most of the Foreign Ministers, &c. at her Apartment in St. James's House"[82]. She even hosted visitors at Kensington Palace, just as any royal wife would. Whether she had actually ever *been* the king's wife is up for debate.

When Walpole wrote that Melusine was "as much Queen of England as ever was", there were those who took that to mean that there had been a secret wedding ceremony between George Louis and Melusine. The king's marriage to Sophia Dorothea of Celle had been dissolved on the grounds of her having abandoned him, leaving him free to remarry in Hanover, and in many ways Melusine would have been the obvious candidate. She had been a faithful and loyal companion for three decades and as César de Saussure observed on his visit to the court, "the King is very fond of her, yet he is not always quite faithful to her, amusing himself

---

81. *British Journal.* 16 February 1723; issue 22.
82. *Daily Journal.* 18 May 1722; issue CCCCXII

with passing intrigues every now and then"[83]. He was a king, after all, infidelity was only the done thing. The couple had children, even if they were publicly acknowledged only as Melusine's nieces, and there is no doubt that everyone at court recognised her sway and influence over the monarch. The question of whether that influence and relationship was ever legitimised by marriage is another matter.

Though George Louis was free to marry Melusine in Hanover immediately upon the dissolution of his marriage to Sophia Dorothea, what was legal in the electorate remained illegal in England. There, no divorced spouse could legally remarry until their former husband or wife was dead and Sophia Dorothea was still very much alive. At the time his marriage ended, George Louis was already aware that he was likely to one day rule in England, so he certainly would have done nothing that might conceivably put this in jeopardy. Duty would always trump love.

There is nothing other than hearsay and rumour to suggest that the couple were married and in truth, with Melusine occupying the rarefied position that she did in George Louis' life, there was little extra to be gained by making the union legitimate. In 1746 Walpole's chaplain, Henry Etough, wrote a letter to a friend in which he claimed that "The late King was expensive and vain in his amours. He had Kilmansegge [sic] and Platen besides Kendal, to whom it is supposed the late Archbishop of York married him."[84] This so-called left-handed or illegitimate marriage would have caused a scandal were it public knowledge, but the fact that it was reported by Etough certainly shouldn't lead to the rumour being accepted as the gospel truth. It's simply impossible to know whether Etough was speaking with authority or repeating some favourite Georgian gossip and gossip, as we have already seen, made the court world go round.

Perhaps, as some have mooted, the fact that Melusine was raised to the rank of princess in the Holy Roman Empire should be taken as an implicit acknowledgement of the marriage, but equally it can be asserted that this was simply a way of recognising her status at the side of the king, whether married to him or not. Regardless of her marital status, by the time Melusine was made a Princess of the Empire, nobody could

---

83. Van Muyden, Madame (ed.) (1902). *A Foreign View of England in the Reigns of George I and George II*. New York: E P Dutton and Company, p.45.

84. Molloy, J Fitzgerald (1897). *Court Life Below Stairs*. London: Downey & Co, Limited, p.52.

challenge her position at court. George Louis trusted her to deal with courtiers and ministers and despite the bitter memory of the South Sea Bubble and the Irish coinage scandal, she remained his closest confidante.

Married or not, the couple had cause to celebrate in late 1721 when George Louis' favourite daughter, Trudchen, married Albrecht Wolfgang, later Count of Schaumburg-Lippe. He was the son of Countess Johanna Sophia of Hohenlohe-Langenburg, who was one of Melusine's best friends, and the marriage was a love match. The two women had met at the electoral court of Hanover, where Johanna Sophia had taken up residence to escape her failing marriage to Count Frederick Christian of Schaumburg-Lippe, and they had been close ever since. Johanna Sophia had accompanied the royal party to England and made her home there, so no doubt she and Melusine were delighted that the union between their children made them as good as family, whilst George Louis was happy to furnish his beloved daughter with a handsome dowry. Though Trudchen's marriage was cut short by her tragic early death, it was a happy one that resulted in two children.

After enduring a bout of colic in 1723, Melusine had more cause than ever to be glad of her influence over the king when trouble broke out during a trip to Hanover. Once again, she would be forced to breathe a sigh of relief that Robert Walpole was the man who held the reins of government. Melusine was about to go head to head with an old rival.

Years earlier, George Louis' rumoured mistress, Sophie Karoline von Platen, sister-in-law of Sophia "the Elephant" Charlotte, had stayed behind in Hanover when the royal party set sail for the new realm. Whilst Melusine was noted approvingly for her work to "repair and Beautify the Swedish church in Trinity-Lane, whither she constantly goes every Sunday"[85], Sophie Karoline's Catholic faith had once made her anxious about the sort of reception she might expect in England. Nearly a decade later, her fears of anti-Catholic sentiment had faded. By 1723, when George Louis and Melusine visited Hanover with Lord Carteret and Lord Townshend, Sophie Karoline was ready to move on.

As Melusine played the hostess at lavish parties and gatherings, Sophie Karoline made a point of getting to know Lord Carteret, who she hoped would be willing and able to smooth her path to a new life in England.

---

85. *Weekly Journal or Saturday's Post*. 12 August 1721; issue 141.

For Robert Walpole and Melusine alike, this was the worst possible news. The existing status quo suited all parties and to have Sophie Karoline suddenly descend on the kingdom and form a breakaway faction with Lord Carteret, who had yet to be packed off to Ireland, would upset the relatively smooth political waters. Melusine didn't want a rival for George Louis' affections either, especially given the acute embarrassment she must have felt when he paid the dowry of Sophie Karoline's daughter, Amalie – a gesture that was sure to ignite rumours regarding the bride's paternity. One shouldn't discount the further humiliation occasioned by the fact that Amalie was engaged to Henri Philippeaux, comte de Florentin, whilst Young Melusine remained unattached.

Walpole, Townshend, and Melusine put their heads together to block the plans of the ambitious countess. Though they couldn't stop George Louis from paying the marriage dowry of Sophie Karoline's daughter, nor from handing over money to Sophie Karoline with the aim of helping her settle in France, they were determined that she would never set foot in England. Her supposed desire to buy a home in Paris was naught but a cover, Walpole and Townshend knew, and it would only be a matter of time before she was causing trouble on British shores.

Just as Walpole, Townshend, and Melusine had their cabal, so too did Sophie Karoline. In her camp she could count Lord Carteret and Christian Ulrich von Hardenberg, one of George Louis' most trusted courtiers and a man of no small ambition. Carteret did all he could to impress Sophie Karoline, even attempting unsuccessfully to have her son-in-law's family raised higher in the French peerage, but his plan backfired. Not only did the Bourbon court resolutely fail to grant his wish, but senior courtiers at Versailles took great offence at his clumsy and unwelcome efforts to manipulate the French royal prerogative. George Louis, acting no doubt on advice from Townshend and Walpole, removed Carteret from his role as Secretary of the Southern Department and made him Lord Lieutenant of Ireland following the removal of the Duke of Grafton. Lord Carteret's days of meddling in Hanoverian marriages were over.

Christian Ulrich von Hardenberg was a different matter. This ambitious politician hoped to be installed by the king as the Prime Minister of Hanover and he made sure to let Melusine know. She would certainly have raised the request with George Louis, and one might expect the promotion to have run its usual steady course, but Hardenberg wasn't willing to wait. His impatience got the better of him and, to Walpole's delight, he made the mistake of discussing his ambitions with Sophie Karoline, who he hoped might have more sway with the king than his aging mistress.

When Melusine learned of Hardenberg's change of allegiance, she was devastated. It was a sign that not everyone believed her influence was ironclad and should Sophie Karoline succeed in joining the English court, then she might look forward to many more such tussles for power. Her discomfort was music to the ears of Walpole and Townshend, to whom Melusine turned for support against Sophie Karoline. Intriguingly, Townshend informed Walpole that Melusine had lobbied so vociferously on Hardenberg's behalf with George Louis that it might even have been to her detriment. That fact made his perceived betrayal all the harder to bear for Melusine, but Townshend encouraged her to continue to make Hardenberg's case to the monarch. If Hardenberg was preoccupied with new duties in Hanover, he reasoned, then that would remove one of Sophie Karoline's chief supporters from the king's immediate presence. The gamble paid off and George Louis was kept so busy with Carteret and Hardenberg that he didn't have time to think about anything else. Sophie Karoline never received an invitation to England.

The king had found the trip to Hanover exhausting and after arriving at the Charlottenburg court of his daughter, Sophia Dorothea, he was taken ill again. By the time he disembarked from the carriage he had been driving, George Louis could barely stand. He collapsed and was bedbound for days. George Louis was no longer a young man and his illness terrified Melusine. She turned to Townshend for help, begging him to convince the king to cancel a planned return to Hanover the following year for the sake of his failing health. Surprisingly for a man who never liked to admit his own weaknesses, the king was happy to cancel. In fact, it was Melusine who fell ill in 1724, not her patron.

By the time the royal entourage set out for Hanover again, there was no annoying Elephant snapping at Melusine's heels. Sophia Charlotte von Kielmansegg, the Duchess of Kendal's rival, died on 20 April 1725. Though Melusine felt little grief at the Countess of Darlington's fate, she was left bereft in 1726 at the death of Margarethe Gertrud, Melusine and George Louis' youngest daughter and by far her father's favourite. *Trudchen* was just 25 years old when she died of tuberculosis. Her father would soon follow her to the grave.

The Widower's Fancy

Three decades after she was locked away behind the walls of Ahlden House, Sophia Dorothea of Celle lingered on the threshold of death. Her life had been comfortable but lonely, one of constant observation and pitifully restricted horizons and now, in the last months of 1726, the mother who had been kept from her children and whose very name was forbidden, drew her last breath. Sophia Dorothea died on 13 November 1726, having spent more than half her lifetime as a prisoner.

George Louis had sent the best doctors that money could buy to tend his ailing former spouse, but to no avail. In the moments before she passed away, Sophia Dorothea supposedly cursed the king's name, damning him. Horace Walpole claimed that a prophet had once "warned George I to take care of his wife, as he would not survive her a year", and that prophecy proved to be true. Walpole slyly theorised that the fanciful rumour had been put about by Sophia Dorothea's parents, who feared that Melusine's ambition might tempt her to arrange the death of their imprisoned daughter, but Melusine wasn't the murdering type.

There was nothing Horace Walpole loved more than to be the man behind the juiciest gossip and at the time of Sophia Dorothea's death he was himself only nine years old. In fact, not long before the king left England for his final trip to Hanover, Horace had seen Melusine's influence first-hand when he had become determined to meet the king. "This childish caprice was so strong," he wrote, "that my mother solicited the Duchess of Kendal to obtain for me the honour of kissing his Majesty's hand before he set out for Hanover."[86] As the son of Robert Walpole the honour was naturally granted and a private audience was arranged for 10.00 pm, on the evening before the sovereign departed for his last journey. Little

---

86. Walpole, Horace (1842). *The Letters Of Horace Walpole, Earl of Orford: Vol* I. Philadelphia: Lea and Blanchard, p.69.

Horace was taken to Melusine's apartments and there kissed the hand of King George I. Melusine, sadly, made little impression.

> "The person of the king is as perfect in my memory as if I saw him but yesterday. It was that of an elderly man, rather pale, and exactly like his pictures and coins; not tall; of an aspect rather good than august; with a dark tie-wig, a plain coat, waistcoat, and breeches of snuff-coloured cloth, with stockings of the same colour, and a blue riband over all. So entirely was he my object that I do not believe I once looked at the duchess; but as I could not avoid seeing her on entering the room, I remember that just beyond his Majesty stood a very tall, lean, ill-favoured old lady; but I did not retain the least idea of her features, nor know what the colour of her dress was."[87]

Melusine was of no interest to the ambitious little courtier, but the death of Sophia Dorothea would *certainly* be of interest to Melusine. As Sophia Dorothea's coffin languished in the vaults at Ahlden awaiting a burial that was delayed by floods, Melusine woke from a nightmare with a terrified start. She told George Louis that his late wife's wrathful spirit had visited her dream to demand that she must be buried in Celle. If that wish were not granted, Sophia Dorothea would never let George Louis rest. Whether the nightmare had anything to do with his decision or not, George Louis swiftly gave his permission for the coffin to be interred in the ducal vault of Celle Castle, where it rests to this day. No monument was erected in memory of Sophia Dorothea.

George Louis forbade all mourning for his former wife and when he heard that his daughter had put her Prussian court into mourning despite his instructions, he was furious. Perhaps feeling his age, perhaps wondering at his apparently declining influence over his family, George Louis reasserted himself by taking a rather unusual decision. He decided to acquire his first and only English mistress. Though Mary Wortley Montagu might have mused that "Monarchs and beauties rule with equal sway" at the court of King George I, in Melusine's case transitory beauty took second place to lifelong companionship. Lifelong companionship, however, occasionally took second place to *amour*.

---

87. Ibid.

The lady George Louis chose to make him feel like a young man again was 20 year old Anne Margaretta Brett, daughter of the scandalous Countess of Macclesfield[88]. One of the court's most striking beauties, Anne knew that bedding the old king would do wonders for her career prospects. George Louis installed Anne in an apartment in St James's Palace and her every wish was his command. When Anne wanted a door to be made in her apartment so that she could directly access the gardens, George Louis had the alteration carried out. The king's granddaughters objected to seeing Anne when they took their walks and commanded that the newly created door be walled up. It was not. That sent a clear signal that Anne Brett was not a lady to be trifled with.

Melusine and George Louis departed for Hanover the day after their meeting with young Horace Walpole. It was to be their last trip together. The passing of Sophia Dorothea of Celle had left the couple free to make their union official at last but if they had any plans to do so, they were never committed to paper nor came to fruition. What Melusine made of Anne Brett we will never know, but Anne fully expected that George Louis would make her a countess when he returned from Hanover. That would have set in stone her place in the second rank, behind Duchess Melusine, but the king was fated never to see England again. Just like Bolingbroke, Mistress Brett was left in the lurch[89].

George Louis spent his last conscious night with Melusine at Delden. Over breakfast the following morning he complained that his sleep had been interrupted by indigestion caused by a supper of strawberries, but he felt sufficiently recovered to travel on. The sea voyage from England had left Melusine unwell and she and George Louis agreed that he would tackle the next leg of the journey alone, leaving her and Young Melusine to follow once she had recovered. The king had always been an early riser and by 7.00 am he was on the road, sharing his carriage with his chamberlain, Friedrich von Fabrice, and Hardenburg. During the journey,

---

88. Anne Brett, Countess of Macclesfield, gave birth to her second illegitimate child by Earl Rivers whilst wearing a mask to conceal her identity and going by the name of Madame Smith. Her husband divorced her but his own bad behaviour was blamed for her decision to take a lover. He was forced to pay back her dowry of £12,000, making Anne a very wealthy woman.
89. Anne contented herself with marriage to William Leman, 3rd Baronet. It was something of a comedown.

George Louis complained of an uncontrollable tremor in his right hand. Minutes later, he suffered a catastrophic stroke.

On his arrival in Osnabrück, George Louis was taken straight to bed. He fell into a deep sleep from which he never awoke, and died just after midnight on 22 June. A messenger was sent to summon Melusine with news of George Louis' collapse and she set out at once for his bedside, only to be intercepted by a second messenger who brought the update that she had been dreading. By the time Melusine and her daughter arrived in Osnabrück early the following day, the king was dead. The news shattered Melusine. She was hysterical with grief.

> "Yesterday arrived an Express, dispatch'd by the Right Hon. The Lord Viscount Townsend [sic], with the melancholy News that his most Excellent Majesty King George fell ill upon the Road to Hanover, and died as Osnabrug [sic] (as we are inform'd) upon which the Guards were doubled. [...] His late Majesty died, very much regretted, in the 68th Year of his Age, and in the 13th of this Reign."[90]

King George I took his last breath on 22 June 1727, just hours before Melusine reached his side. As the prophet had supposedly predicted, George Louis did not survive Sophia Dorothea by a year. Soon the unhappy event had been given a Gothic rewrite, with unfounded tales spreading that a black-garbed rider on an ebony steed had thrust a deathbed curse written by Sophia Dorothea through the window of the king's carriage. As soon as he read it, so the story went, George Louis collapsed.

Melusine was heartbroken. She had lost the man who had been her rock for thirty years and as the funeral plans were made in Hanover, she drew her surviving daughters close. George Louis was laid to rest in the chapel of the Leineschloss[91]. For the first time in three decades, the Duchess of Kendal was alone.

---

90. *Daily Post*. 15 June 1727; issue 2411.
91. When Allied bombs destroyed the Leineschloss during the Second World War, the remains of George I were moved to Herrenhausen, where they rest to this day.

After George

"[George I] was rather a good sort of man than a shining king," wrote Horace Walpole in his *Reminiscences*, "And, as the duchess [sic] of Kendal was no genius, I heard very little of either when he and her power were no more."[92] Walpole wasn't alone, and when George Louis died, Melusine quietly assumed a different sort of life. The Duchess of Kendal became an English gentlewoman.

The *British Journal* reported in late June that "A House is hired in Park place [sic] in St. James's-street for the Duchess of Kendal and the Countess of Walsingham, who are daily expected from Osnaburg,"[93] but the expectation that Melusine and her daughter would be back in England anytime soon proved to be a false one. Instead the grieving duchess elected to remain in Hanover until the coronation of George II had taken place. Melusine was not the king's widow and had never been his queen. It was better that she take her time to say goodbye. Soon the updates on her expected arrival in England changed to stories of a serious turn in her health and even false reports of her death. In truth, Melusine was utterly bereft.

Melusine had no wish to be reminded of all that she had lost and in George's ancestral lands, where he now rested, she could at least be close to her late partner in some small way. What awaited her in England now, she couldn't say. Melusine's relationship with George II was pleasant enough and she was on good terms with his wife, Caroline of Ansbach, but beyond that the world had suddenly become a very uncertain place for the Duchess of Kendal. With the passing of her companion, the man she undoubtedly loved and had, despite his grumpy ways, loved her in return, Melusine's life had changed forever.

---

92. Walpole, Horace (1818). *Lord Orford's Reminiscences*. London: John Sharpe, p.4.
93. *British Journal*. 24 June 1727; issue 248.

As 1727 drew to a close Melusine was still unwell, but she had recovered sufficiently to purchase "an [sic] House of about 5000l. near Hanover-Square."[94] It was to this house that Melusine, Young Melusine and Luise withdrew. When winter turned to spring, they retired to Kendal House, a newly built residence on the banks of the Thames at Isleworth. Here Melusine lived a quiet life, for what influence could she offer ambitious politicians now?

Melusine sold off her estate in Holstein for a handsome profit, and she received a sum of nearly £22,000 in the late king's will. In addition to this, she received a further £7,000 that George Louis had left in trust to keep his companion comfortable should he predecease her. This money went partially to fund a dowry for Young Melusine when she married Philip Dormer Stanhope, 4th Earl of Chesterfield, and partly towards the bill for Kendal House. Despite her marriage, Young Melusine continued to live with her mother whilst her husband indulged his mistresses in London.

The elder Melusine, meanwhile, faded from the public consciousness as swiftly as she had entered it. Once the closest thing to a queen that England would see during the reign of George I, now the only excitement that punctuated her routine days was the breaking of a mirror. It was still enough to occupy the press, but it was hardly the South Sea Bubble.

"Yesterday, as two Porters were carrying thro' St. Martin's Church-Yard, a Pier Glass about 5 Foot long, belonging to her Grace the Dutchess [sic] of Kendal, a Boy passing by with a Two Quart Pot in his Hand, clapt the Pot on the Glass, and broke it into several Pieces: He was carried before a Justice of the Peace, who send him to the Round House, till his Friends should make good the damage."[95]

But Melusine didn't concern herself with such trifling matters. She was too busy ruing all that she had lost. Years earlier, if legend is to be believed, George Louis had promised Melusine that even death couldn't part them. Now, with George Louis gone and Melusine alone at Isleworth, Horace Walpole claimed that the king's promise had unexpectedly come true. As Melusine watched the world go by from Kendal House, a vast black

94. *Weekly Journal or British Gazetteer.* 30 December 1727; issue 138.
95. *Daily Journal.* 24 April 1730; issue 2901.

raven supposedly flew through an open window and settled beside her. From that day forward the raven reputedly became Melusine's constant companion. Once the candles were extinguished and the house fell silent, she could be heard talking to the pampered bird about her day, just as she and the king had once whiled away the evenings together in her royal apartments.

Whether the story of the raven is true is debateable, but the best legends often are. Horace Walpole was an inveterate teller of tales and this one, Gothic and romantic, feels like something from one of his novels. True or not though, Melusine mourned her lost king for the rest of her life.

The Death of the Duchess

"Last Tuesday Evening about 7 o'clock died, at her house in Grosvenor-Square, after a few Days Illness, her Grace Erengard-Melusina Schuylenberg [sic], Princess of Eberstein, Dutchess [sic] of Kendal and Munster, Marchioness and Countess of Dungannon, Countess of Faversham, and Baroness of Schuylenberg, Dundalk and Glastonbury."[96]

Melusine died at the age of 75 on 10 May 1743. When Horace Walpole recorded her death he mistakenly noted that she was 85 years old, but he was right when he told Horace Mann that "her riches were immense, but I believe my Lord Chesterfield will get nothing by her death but his wife". Melusine had never liked her son-in-law, or the way he treated her daughter after their marriage. Chesterfield believed that his mother-in-law was "very little above an idiot," but she was certainly canny enough to ensure that the money she left to Young Melusine could not be seized by her husband.

In her will, Melusine distributed her wealth to her daughters Melusine, Countess of Chesterfield, and Luise, Countess of Dölitz, who had never remarried following her divorce – there was far too much fun to be had for that. Melusine was laid to rest in a private vault at South Audley Street Chapel. Melusine and George Louis' surviving daughters, Luise and Young Melusine, died in 1773 and 1778 respectively. They were interred alongside their mother and with that, the vault was sealed. The story of Melusine von der Schulenberg, the longest-serving mistress of any of the Georgian kings, had come to an end.

---

96. *London Evening Post*. 10 May 1743–12 May 1743; issue 2419.

Act II

Henrietta Howard, Countess of Suffolk

(c. 1689–26 July 1767)

The Daughter of Blickling Hall

The little girl who was to become one of the most famous faces of the Georgian court was born in 1689 to a family who occupied an illustrious if crumbling address. Henrietta Hobart was one of eight children born to Sir Henry Hobart, 4th Baronet, and his wife, Elizabeth, who lived at Blickling Hall[97] in Norfolk. Sir Henry Hobart had inherited from his father not only the debt-ridden family estate at Blickling Hall, but also the unofficial position of leader of the Norfolk Whigs. He was a well-connected career politician who served as a Gentleman of the Horse for William III and fought with the king's forces at the Battle of the Boyne, but despite his other successes, he had no head for money. Marriage to the wealthy Elizabeth Maynard went some way to temporarily holding off Sir Henry's creditors, but as the years passed, his parlous finances fell once again into wrack and ruin as the ancestral pile and expensive election campaigns cleaned him out. Sir Henry's life was beset with challenges and he was in and out of parliament for nearly two decades, riding a roller coaster of success and defeat.

Young Henrietta knew none of this. Instead her early life was quiet, uneventful, and totally in keeping with that of a daughter of a seventeenth century aristocrat. She was trained in the female arts from a young age, and she was prepared for the good and profitable marriage that, her parents no doubt hoped, would be her destiny.

Fate had other things in store for the Hobart family though, and Henrietta's idyllic childhood was shattered in 1698 when her father lost his Norfolk seat in parliament to Sir William Cook. It wasn't a close-run thing either, for he was roundly beaten into third place and flung unceremoniously out of office. Sir Henry was furious. He had given years of his life and a fortune in family money to the pursuit of politics and,

---

97. Blickling Hall was believed to have been the birthplace of Queen Anne Boleyn and according to legend, her restless spirit walks there still.

just like that, he was finished. At the time of the election the political atmosphere was nothing short of toxic, and even as Sir Henry was spending a king's ransom failing to secure his seat, rumours that he had behaved with cowardice at the Battle of the Boyne began to circulate. There could be few greater insults than this.

Sir Henry blamed the damaging rumours for his defeat, and he blamed his outspoken Tory neighbour, Oliver Le Neve, for the rumours. Determined to seek redress, he challenged his neighbour to a duel "for spreading a report that he was a coward and behaved himself so in Ireland, by which 'tis said he lost his election for the county."[98] If the man behind the gossip was a true gentleman, said Sir Henry, then he would agree to the duel as a matter of honour. At first Le Neve protested his innocence, but Sir Henry wouldn't be placated. When he issued a second challenge, Le Neve told him that if the accusation wasn't withdrawn, then he would consent to the duel if only to clear his name. Le Neve would certainly have been wary of facing his neighbour, but honour was honour and must be restored.

The two men met on Cawston Heath on 20 August 1698 to engage in the last duel ever fought on Norfolk soil. Because duelling was illegal by then, no seconds accompanied them just in case the meeting led to criminal proceedings. The weapon of choice was swords. Sir Henry made the first move and struck Le Neve in the arm, but with an answering thrust Le Neve's sword pierced Sir Henry Hobart's stomach, inflicting a deep laceration. That was the end of the duel and the badly-bleeding Sir Henry withdrew. Mortally wounded, he fled for Blickling Hall where his agonised cries echoed around the corridors. He died the following day.

"Yesterday's post brought us an account of poor Sir Harry Hobart's death. He received his wound on Saturday and died on Sunday night; they say he sent the challenge to Le Neve, one of the militia captains, who had reported him a coward. Le Neve declined the first challenge but complied with the second; he is likewise hurt in two or three places, but not mortally."[99]

---

98. Luttrell, Narcissus (1857). *A Brief Historical Relation of State Affaires from September 1678 to April 1714: Vol IV*. Oxford: Oxford University Press, p.418.
99. Vernon, James (1841). *Letters Illustrative of the Reign of William III from 1696 to 1708: Vol II*. London: Henry Colburn, p.158.

When Whig statesman James Vernon coolly reported the death of Sir Henry Hobart in in the above letter to the Duke of Shrewsbury, his words little hinted at the turmoil that had been whipped up by the duel. Fearing the repercussions of the killing, Oliver Le Neve fled Norfolk for London and began what would become an arduous life on the run. Sir Henry's widow, Lady Elizabeth, promised a £500 reward to anyone who could capture her husband's killer and, with the Norfolk Militia hot on his trail, Le Neve escaped England and headed for Rotterdam. Once her husband had been laid to rest at Blickling Hall, Lady Elizabeth erected a monument to his memory on the very spot where he had suffered his fatal wound. It stands there to this day. Le Neve remained on the continent for two years in the hope of evading justice, but a trial was held during his absence nonetheless.

> "On Saturday last Mr. Le Neve was tried for killing Sir Henry Hobart at Thetford and was found Guilty of Manslaughter."[100]

When a broken and desperate Le Neve eventually returned to England to face the music, he was put on trial in person before a grand jury. This time he was acquitted.

When Sir Henry Hobart died, he left "his affairs [in] a confused condition, and his two brothers almost destitute; he had eight children, a great debt upon his estate, and law entanglements upon his wife's fortunes." In short, Sir Henry left a mess.[101] At just four years old, the Hobart son and heir, John, was too young to take on the tangled affairs of Blickling so that unenviable job passed to Elizabeth, the grieving widow. She was the daughter of politician Sir Joseph Maynard and had come into the marriage with an enormous dowry of £10,000, which her husband had swiftly spent. Now she was saddled with a crumbling family pile and debts that she couldn't hope to repay. The basic upkeep of Blickling Hall generated more and more debt every single day and with her financial challenges so well known to all and sundry, the chances of snaring a rich husband to plug the gaps were close to zero. Nobody wanted Lady Elizabeth if the money pit that was Blickling Hall was part of the deal.

---

100. *Post Boy*. 21 March 1700–23 March 1700; issue 773.
101. Vernon, James (1841). *Letters Illustrative of the Reign of William III from 1696 to 1708: Vol II*. London: Henry Colburn, p.158.

There was only one way that Elizabeth could turn. Her twice widowed step-great-grandmother, Mary Howard, had made an excellent third marriage to the 5th Earl of Suffolk[102] and it was to this illustrious branch on the family tree that Lady Elizabeth now appealed for help. To her delight and surprise, the Countess of Suffolk invited her and the Hobart children to be her guests at Gunnersbury House in West London, which she had inherited from her late husband, Elizabeth's hugely wealthy great-grandfather, Sir John Maynard. For Lady Elizabeth and her family, the trip was a welcome change of pace.

Lady Elizabeth and her children passed the summer of 1699 at Gunnersbury House, pampered and tended to in a manner befitting the household of the Earl of Suffolk. It became a sanctuary, but it was soon to be marred by tragedy.

In the summer of 1701, Lady Elizabeth fell ill during a visit to Gunnersbury. She died that summer of consumption, leaving her orphaned children behind. Things could hardly get any worse. The ailing Blickling estates were in the hands of trustees until John came of age but when it came to day-to-day life, the Hobart children looked to their eldest siblings to care for them. The following years brought with them tragedy after tragedy. In quick succession, the eldest three Hobart daughters died, until 16-year-old Henrietta reached the front of the queue. Her childhood was over.

The year was 1705, and things were more desperate than ever. All but alone and facing an endless struggle against the debts her father had left behind, Henrietta made a decision that would change her life forever. When she was invited to stay at Gunnersbury House on a semi-permanent basis, she said yes.

---

102. Mary had a habit of making good marriages. She started with Sir Charles Vermuyden, moved onto Sir John Maynard – Henrietta's great-grandfather – and finally plumped for the Earl of Suffolk.

Marrying Suffolk

When Henrietta went to the Howards for help, it is likely that the desperate young woman would have accepted virtually any offer they might have made. She was in dire straits, worn down by the seemingly endless round of bereavements and the grind of life at Blickling Hall. Protected from the worst of her father's spending excesses by her mother, Henrietta's life had once been idyllic. Now it was drudgery.

In the care of the Howards though, Henrietta could forget her cares for a while and enjoy a more laid-back pace of life. Both at Gunnersbury House and Audley End, their palatial residence near Saffron Walden, the elderly Earl Henry Howard and his wife, Mary, lived the sort of life that only substantial wealth could bring. Henry had been widowed twice before he married Mary and had managed to achieve a rather unusual hattrick in that all three of his wives were named Mary. The first of the Marys, Mary Stewart, had borne her husband three sons, each of whom would eventually take their turn as the holder of the title, Earl of Suffolk. They were Henry, born in 1670, Edward, born in 1672, and Charles, born in 1675.[103]

Before he had reached 30 years old, Charles Howard had already achieved the rank of Captain in Lord Echlin's Regiment of Dragoons and sat in the Irish House of Commons. His military career was solid rather than glittering, and he won the praise of his peers and climbed the ranks at a respectable pace. Respectable was the last word one would use to describe his private life. The Earl of Chesterfield dismissed him as "sour, dull and sullen,"[104] but perhaps we should defer to Baron Hervey,

---

103. Henry, Edward, and Charles were respectively the 6th, 8th and 9th Earls of Suffolk. Edward succeeded to the title on the death of Henry's only son and heir, Charles, who died in 1722 having been 7th Earl of Suffolk for less than four years. He was 29 years old.

104. Mahon, Lord (ed.) (1845). *The Letters of Philip Dormer Stanhope, Earl of Chesterfield: Vol II*. London: Richard Bentley, p.440.

that incorrigible chronicler of George II's court, for Charles' most searing character reference. Hervey always spoke as he found, and he described Charles Howard not as a battlefield hero or some sort of dashing young noble, but as the "wrong-headed, ill tempered, obstinate, drunken, extravagant, brutal younger brother of the Earl of Suffolk's family."[105] Henrietta would see all of these unenviable qualities over the years of their marriage.

Though Hervey could be guilty of a waspishness that bordered on brutal, in the case of Charles Howard he could not be accused of doing the man a disservice. Charles was a violent womaniser with twin addictions to alcohol and gambling. He drank and whored his way through his allowance and army pay, but when the need arose, he could turn on a devastatingly disarming charm. Perhaps it was this charm that blinded 16-year-old Henrietta to his flaws when he arrived at Gunnersbury and found her living under the roof of his elderly father and his glamourous stepmother. Henrietta was young, intelligent, and no doubt breathing a sigh of relief that the Howards had rescued her from Blickling Hall, where her siblings remained under the care of the household staff. At 16, she was also ripe for marriage. Henrietta had begun her education in how to be a gentlewoman at an early age and ably combined all the qualities necessary in a society wife. At Blickling Hall the pickings for a bridegroom would be spare indeed but with the Earl and Countess of Suffolk to guide her through society, the field of candidates might reliably be expected to far exceed that available in Norfolk.

Whoever won Henrietta's hand could look forward to receiving a very handsome dowry as well as an inheritance from her immensely wealthy great-grandfather, Sir John Maynard, that was being held in trust until she married. No doubt Henrietta had plans of her own when it came to her siblings, and a good marriage to a rich husband could do wonders for their prospects too. It was vital that she marry and marry well.

To the Earl and Countess, the orphaned Henrietta might well have seemed heaven-sent to take the youngest, most troublesome Howard son off their hands. How the romance came to be is lost to history but

---

105. Croker, John Wilson (ed.) (1848). *Memoirs of the Reign of George II from his Accession to the Death of Queen Caroline by John, Lord Hervey: Vol I.* London: John Murray, p.54.

we can be sure that Charles Howard certainly turned up his charm to the maximum and toned down the side of him that threw good money after bad at the gaming tables or roared drunk around the cities, pursuing women and trouble with equal ardour. Sheltered, worn-down by cares beyond her years, and ready for a comfortable life, Henrietta was bowled over by the worldly older man, and the Howards were happy to encourage the romance. After all, a marriage would mean that Charles would become someone else's problem and when he did, he'd scoop up all that money that was being held in trust for the day Henrietta tied the knot. Before long, the match was made and Henrietta was preparing for life as Mrs Charles Howard, little knowing what she was getting herself into.

Although Henrietta was orphaned, she wasn't entirely alone in the world. One of her uncles practised law and, luckily for the young bride-to-be, he took the matter of his late brother's finances far more seriously than he did that of his late brother's children. He drew up a marriage settlement that protected most of Henrietta's money from her avaricious husband. It also guaranteed her an income for her personal expenses from the interest on a sum of £6,000 that was held in trust. Charles had no legal right to either the lump sum or the interest it earned, though he would bully and coerce Henrietta into handing her money over to him throughout their marriage. Legally though, he had no claim on the cash and should his wife die – or perhaps meet with an unfortunate accident – the money would still not be given to Charles. Instead, it would be held in trust until the couple's children reached adulthood.

The happy couple were wed on 2 March 1706 at St Benet Paul's Wharf, the official church of the College of Arms. Soon afterwards Charles sold off his army commission for £700, a sum that no doubt slipped through his fingers as readily as grains of sand. Henrietta's honeymoon period swiftly came to an abrupt end.

Mr and Mrs Smith

With the wedding out of the way, the newlyweds settled into London life and Henrietta was soon expecting what was to be her first and only child. Yet the marriage quickly soured, and she must have rued the youthful enthusiasm that led her to accept the worldly and cunning Charles Howard's proposal. The Earl of Chesterfield summed up the unhappy situation that followed the hasty marriage when he wrote, "thus they loved, thus they married, and thus they hated each other for the rest of their lives."[106]

Though Henrietta's uncle had drawn up a marriage settlement that should have protected her interests, once the front door closed and the couple was alone, that was easier said than done. Charles burned through his own money and then started on his wife's, spending it as though it was a well that would never run dry. Soon he was back to his old ways, drinking, gambling, fighting, and wenching, and his pregnant wife was abandoned back at home, fearful of her new husband's brutal temper. Though he couldn't get his hands on her money legally, he could do it by menace instead and Charles soon relieved Henrietta of the allowance that was meant for her personal expenses. The money proved nowhere near enough to meet his needs and he went so far as to bring a suit in the Court of Chancery against his wife's trustees, hoping to lay claim to the entire £6,000 which provided Henrietta with her income. The suit failed, which further blackened relations between the Howards. When Henrietta gave birth to a son on New Year's Day 1707, what should have been a day of unbridled happiness no doubt came tempered with new worries for the unhappy woman. Little Henry Howard was just one more mouth to feed.

---

106. Mahon, Lord (ed.) (1845). *The Letters of Philip Dormer Stanhope, Earl of Chesterfield: Vol II*. London: Richard Bentley, p.440.

If living the high life in London with a wife in tow was a pain for Charles, living the high life with a new baby at home was something he wasn't prepared to countenance. He packed mother and baby off to a miserable set of lodgings in Berkshire, where Henrietta experienced the most poverty-stricken days she had ever known. For more than two years the couple lived apart, one in misery, one in debt-ridden hedonism, and Charles saw his infant son only a handful of times. He had married for money and with Henrietta's income lining his pockets for as long as he could refrain from gambling it away, Charles Howard's wife and child could be forgotten. Naturally, Charles saw the situation somewhat differently. Far from being the author of Henrietta's misfortune, the man who had a reputation for trouble long before they married actually blamed her for his penury. Later in the marriage he furiously spat "you had a share in former years from him who was not a beggar when he first knew you", as though Henrietta had been the one to wring *him* dry. It was very much the other way round. Charles might not have been a beggar when they met, but he was certainly well-travelled along the road to ruin.

Yet whilst it was Charles who racked up debt after debt, it was Henrietta who suffered. What few possessions she had managed to cling onto were seized by Charles' creditors and after a couple of years living a miserable life in Berkshire, Henrietta was evicted from her sorry lodgings when she was no longer able to pay the rent. She couldn't even go back to London, for the modest city home she had shared so briefly with Charles after their marriage was also lost to them, thanks to her husband's gambling.

When Charles' father died in 1709 his brother, Henry, became 6th Earl of Suffolk. It was to him that the little family now appealed for help. He grudgingly offered them a home at Audley End, but there was to be no charity. The family would have to pay rent. Henrietta and little Henry remained at Audley End for two years whilst Charles continued his self-destructive life in London, but Henrietta was still determined to try and make a go of the marriage, despite all that she had suffered at his hands. She left Audley End and went back to the city, where she took up residence with her husband in Covent Garden until the money ran out. Occasionally adopting the pseudonym *Smith* to escape Charles' creditors, the family moved from place to place around the city to keep one step ahead of their debts, each new destination more hopeless than the last.

If Henrietta had been hoping to somehow reform Charles, she was soon disavowed of that notion. She was poor, hungry, and hopeless, abused, ignored, and kept as a household servant for a man who had no affection or regard for either his wife or their son. Something had to change.

The Heir of Hanover

As Charles Howard was working his charms on young Henrietta in 1705, far away at the electoral court of Hanover there was another young man thinking of marriage. He was George Augustus, son of George Louis and his unfortunate wife, Sophia Dorothea of Celle. Perhaps because his own marriage to Sophia Dorothea had ended so horribly, George Louis was determined that he wouldn't impose a bride on his son without letting George Augustus have some say in the matter too.

Dowager Electress Sophia, George I's formidable and well-connected mother, had long since decided that Princess Caroline of Ansbach would make the ideal wife for her grandson. Following the death of first her father then her mother after a brutal second marriage, Caroline had been raised at the Prussian court by the king and queen, Frederick I of Prussia, and Sophia Charlotte of Hanover, George Louis' sister. As a friend of Caroline's late mother, Sophia Charlotte was more than happy to take the orphaned girl into her household and raised her as though she was her own daughter. Princess Caroline was young, well brought up and, crucially, Protestant. She was also intelligent, cultured and entirely unpolitical, or so the Hanoverian contingent believed. History would prove them very wrong on that score.

With his family poised to one day sit on the British throne, George Augustus was one of the most eligible bachelors on the continent, and both he and his father were keenly aware of the fact that the young man would make a tempting prospect indeed for any would-be brides with ambition. For that reason, they came up with a plan to let the couple meet without telling Caroline that George was in fact heir to the electorate of Hanover, not to mention the throne of Great Britain. Only then could they be sure that she wanted George Augustus for the right reasons, rather than financial ones.

Sophia Charlotte of Hanover died in February 1705, plunging the Prussian court into mourning. It was still in mourning for its late queen when George Augustus paid a visit to Triesdorf that summer. He arrived without ceremony and was travelling under the assumed name of Monsieur de Busch, ostensibly to ensure that the 22-year-old Caroline had no idea who he was. Whether she had seen through his subterfuge or not must remain a mystery but as the summer progressed, the young couple fell head over heels for each other. It was a fairy tale romance and when Caroline learned of her suitor's true identity, she professed to be stunned. By then George Augustus and Caroline of Ansbach were in love, and they were married on 2 September 1705. It sounds like a fairy tale, but we must ask whether Caroline knew who Monsieur de Busch was all along. She very probably did, but it doesn't make for such a good legend.

All of this was watched with interest by the most ambitious and well-connected English courtiers. It was by now virtually guaranteed that the electoral family was destined to rule Britain when the still childless Queen Anne died, and every courtier wanted to be the new monarch's favourite when that moment came. Dowager Electress Sophia and George Louis weren't about to come to England to meet them, so those who sought advancement decided that they should go to Hanover instead. If the streets weren't quite paved with gold, then at least dreams might come true at the hands of the Hanoverians.

Money and hangers-on poured into Hanover and amongst those who watched with growing interest was the miserable Henrietta Howard. If she could only finance a trip to the continent, she was sure that she would be able to turn her family fortunes around at the electoral court of George Louis. When Henrietta told Charles of her plans, he enthusiastically supported them, though he did nothing to fund the trip. Henrietta sold what few possessions she could still call her own and squirrelled away the money in her travelling fund. How heartbreaking it must have been when Charles stole that meagre travelling fund and gambled it away.

Now the Howards truly had nothing except Henrietta's little income from her trust fund. Once again she began to hide her money away, living in poverty whilst her errant husband plunged deeper than ever into vice. He had so little care for his wife that she was reduced to trying to sell her own hair to a wigmaker, but when she was offered the derisory sum of eighteen guineas, she resolved to keep it instead. When Henrietta told Charles about the pittance that the wigmaker had offered for her crowning glory, he mocked her reticence and said he was only surprised she had received such a generous offer. Henrietta was thoroughly humiliated, but though life at home might be miserable, her cherished plans to go to Hanover and secure a comfortable future for her little boy gave her something to focus on. Every single penny went into the pot until she had reached her target, but even then, there was something else that was playing on Henrietta's mind.

Ever since the birth of Henry Howard seven years earlier, the only constant in his life had been his mother. The little boy's father had been mostly absent, and he had been dragged from slum to slum, sometimes under an assumed name, living in penury and waiting for the next heavy knock at the door. Henrietta's meagre savings would only pay for two to go to Hanover, and there was no possibility of leaving Charles behind. Whoever she entrusted with the care of Henry is unknown, but it's likely that she appealed once more to the Howards of Audley End for help. She would certainly have known the little boy would be safe with his paternal family.

Once she had said goodbye to her son, Henrietta packed what few things she still possessed and she and Charles began the journey to Hanover, where George Louis and Melusine sat at the head of the court. Henrietta little knew it at the time, but it was his son with whom she would make the biggest splash.

A New Beginning

When Henrietta and Charles reached Hanover, they were destitute once more. If the plan to win the trust and patronage of the electoral court failed, then the future looked bleak indeed. They had no money to fall back on and every penny received from Henrietta's allowance was plunged straight into the pockets of their creditors unless Charles got to it first. If he did, then it went into the coffers of the nearest brothel or was lost at the gaming tables or drunk away in a London tavern. By now Henrietta was "of a just height, well made, extremely fair, with the finest light-brown hair; was remarkably genteel, and always well dressed with taste and simplicity."[107] She would be an ornament to any court gathering, and she had the manners, pedigree and intelligence to match.

The English visitors were made very welcome indeed when they arrived at the court of Hanover and though it was Dowager Electress Sophia who was first in line to the throne, she knew as well as anyone that she was unlikely to inherit it. By now she was in her eighties and Queen Anne, the current incumbent, was only in her forties, so Sophia was certain that she would predecease Anne by some considerable years. The ambitious English who flocked to Hanover suspected it too, so they made it their business to ingratiate themselves with George Louis and his son as well as Sophia. After all, there was no point being favoured by the mother if her son and heir didn't even know your name. Henrietta intended to make the Howards indispensable to both.

Once she and her husband had found humble rooms in Hanover, Henrietta went to Herrenhausen whilst Charles slunk off to sample the hedonistic delights that the electorate could offer. Henrietta was granted an audience with Sophia, who had always valued rank and title and was happy to meet the in-law of an earl. Despite her reduced circumstances,

---

107. Walpole, Horace (1842). *The Letters of Horace Walpole, Earl of Orford: Vol I.* Philadelphia: Lea and Blanchard, p.95.

Henrietta had pedigree to spare and she could complement that with a pleasing character and keen mind. She was, in short, just the kind of woman that the electress had always found charming company and once she was admitted to Sophia's inner circle, Henrietta made herself an indispensable attendant. Let's not forget that it was Henrietta to whom Sophia mocked Melusine as "that tall mawkin", a sure sign that she was a trusted friend of the family. Acceptance by Sophia meant that a similar friendship from Caroline of Ansbach was swift to follow. Sophia adored her granddaughter-in-law and Caroline loved her in turn, so Henrietta found herself with two champions at Herrenhausen. Under Sophia of Hanover's wing, she had seemingly found her place.

But there was still a fly named Charles in the ointment. It was one thing for Henrietta to be carving out a position at Sophia's side, but if the Howards were to enjoy continued favour then Charles would need to turn on his charm once more. He too would need to find a position. Whilst Henrietta, Sophia and Caroline had much in common to discuss, the hedonistic Charles and the dour elector had precious few shared interests. Worse still, though Sophia loved the attention that the English paid to her, George Louis was far from fond of them. He regarded them as fortune seekers who sought his favours only for the sake of their own ambition, so perhaps that's why he fell for the earthy charms of Charles Howard. Whatever it was, soon the elector and Henrietta's husband were unlikely friends. Even better, George Louis and Sophia assured Charles and Henrietta that there would be positions waiting for them when the Hanoverians assumed the British throne.

Of course, there was one other person in Hanover to whom Henrietta would endear herself. That was George Augustus, the son of the elector and the husband of Caroline, who had so welcomed Henrietta into her coterie. The sociable and outgoing George Augustus was more his mother's son than his father's and he was just as charmed by Henrietta as his grandmother Sophia had been. The dowager watched the growing intimacy between the two with a wry amusement, commenting only, "It will improve his English". She had always known when to be discreet.

At what point the intimacy between George Augustus and his wife's attendant became something more than platonic has been the subject of debate for decades. No correspondence remains to give us a clue, but when one considers Henrietta's priorities at this stage in her life, I think it's unlikely that she and George Augustus were lovers before they left Hanover for England. Besides, George Augustus had other favourites amongst his wife's circle. Henrietta was far from being at the front of the line.

The Howards had been at the Hanoverian court for approximately a year when tragedy struck. Dowager Electress Sophia died in her beloved garden at Herrenhausen and her son George Louis took her place as next in line to the British throne. A matter of weeks later Queen Anne died, and Henrietta's life was to change once again.

At Court

"On Thursday last Queen Anne was taken very ill, at her Palace at Kensington, and so continu'd all that Day; the next Morning her Majesty was seiz'd with Convulsions, which went off for Some Hours; so that Some Small Hopes were conceiv'd of her Recovery, but on Sunday after Seven in the morning She departed this Life. Hereupon the Lords of the Council met at St. James's, and issu'd a Proclamation, importing, That by the Decease of her late Majesty Queen Anne, of blessed Memory, the Imperial Crowns of Great Britain, France, and Ireland, and solely and rightfully come to the High and Mighty Prince George, elector of Brunswick-Luneburg."[108]

When Henrietta and Charles Howard left England, they were hopeless, destitute, and on their very last chance. They returned as members of the new king's coterie. Henrietta's gamble had more than paid off. Perhaps best of all, a return to her homeland meant that Henrietta could finally be reunited with her beloved son, Henry.

Bad weather delayed the departure of the new king's party but eventually they set off from The Hague for the kingdom that George Louis now ruled. Amongst the party was George Augustus, whilst Caroline of Ansbach and the couple's daughters were to follow a month later. Their eldest son, Frederick, stayed behind in Hanover to serve as the family figurehead.

The royal family made their new home at St James's Palace and all those courtiers who had flocked to Hanover to win their favour now found that they had to repeat the feat in England. Official appointments were being made and nobody wanted to miss out because they were slow to leave Hanover, least of all the Howards, who had pinned all their hopes

108. *British Mercury.* 28 July 1714–4 August 1714; issue 474.

for the future on the new monarch and his family. Henrietta and her husband weren't part of the initial group who sailed for England, but they weren't far behind. As soon as she arrived in London Henrietta made for St James's and an audience with Caroline of Ansbach, who was the highest-ranking woman at court since George Louis no longer had a wife or a mother. Thankfully, Caroline remembered the promise she had made to Henrietta Howard and gave her the position of Woman of the Bedchamber, as "Mrs. Howard had had a Promise of it from *Hanover* in the Princess *Sophia's* Time"[109]. Charles too was awarded with an appointment and became Groom of the Bedchamber to George I.

The appointments weren't merely ceremonial either, and each brought with it several duties. As a Woman of the Bedchamber, Henrietta was expected to attend the Princess of Wales at her toilet, assisting with her bathing, dressing and other personal matters. A Woman of the Bedchamber was inferior in rank to a Lady of the Bedchamber, usually the wife or widow of a peer, all of whom were presided over by the First Lady of the Bedchamber and Groom of the Stole. In the household of Caroline of Ansbach at the time of Henrietta's appointment, this lofty position was occupied by Diana Beauclerk, Duchess of St Albans. Also among the women was young Molly Lepell, George I's particular favourite until Melusine paid her to make herself scarce, and a lady named Mary Bellenden, who soon won the affections of George Augustus. As far as the balladeers were concerned, they were the fairest ladies at court by a long way.

> "So well I'm known at Court
> None asks where Cupid dwells;
> But readily resort
> To Bellenden's or Lepell's."

As a Groom of the Bedchamber Charles theoretically had similar duties to perform for George I to those his carried out by his wife for the Princess of Wales. However, George Louis preferred to rely on the German servants who had attended him for years, meaning that Charles' role required

---

109. Cowper, Mary (1865). *Diary of Mary Countess Cowper, Lady of the Bedchamber to the Princess of Wales, 1714 -1720*. London: John Murray, p.26.

little work indeed. It might have been tailormade for him, but the same couldn't be said for Henrietta's position. Caroline worked her Women of the Bedchamber hard, and they spent hours each day waiting on her from the moment she woke to the moment she retired for the evening. In fact, the Women of the Bedchamber were hard at work long before their mistress left her bed, preparing her toilette and clothes for the day ahead. It was an arduous role, entirely subject to the whims of the princess.

In a world in which such appointments were ruthlessly fought over, it was an achievement that the Howards were proud of. Even better for the couple who had once scurried from one hovel to another, the roles brought with them both a wage and apartments in St James's Palace, a necessity for those who held positions in the bedchamber. Though apartments in a palace might sound grand, St James's Palace had seen better days. It was gloomy, damp and filled to overflowing with the new court, but it must have seemed luxurious to Henrietta after some of the dire places in which her husband's debts had forced her to reside. For the first time in years, Henrietta could finally allow herself to breathe.

What she couldn't allow herself to do was shirk. Though Charles' master preferred his German servants to his newly appointed Grooms of the Bedchamber, the Princess of Wales wasn't about to let her ladies off so easily. They were required to be available whenever she needed them and though it was a far cry from the drudgery of Henrietta's early days with her husband, it was still anything but easy. We shouldn't lull ourselves into the belief that Henrietta bore it all without complaint though. After chatting to Henrietta during a visit to the royal household, her friend Alexander Pope wryly noted that he and Henrietta had "agreed that the life of a Maid of Honor was of all things the most miserable, & wished that every Woman who envyd it had a Specimen of it. To eat Westphalia Ham in a morning, ride over Hedges and ditches on borrowed Hacks, [then] simper an hour, & catch cold, in the Princesses [sic] apartment; from thence *to Dinner* [and] after that, till midnight, walk, work, or think, which they please"[110]. It wasn't a life for the fainthearted, but neither was marriage to Charles Howard.

There was also the ever-present matter of court drama and among the ladies of the household, politics was as important as it was in the chamber

---

110. *Corr.*, I, 427.

of the House of Commons itself. Just as Melusine had done her best to avoid squabbles and politicking in Hanover, so too did Henrietta attempt to keep out of it in England. She had made it as far as the royal inner circle and she had no wish to jeopardise her position, which only served to make her more popular than ever amongst her comrades in the bedchamber. Henrietta could be trusted, they intuited, and was beyond the conniving ways of some of her peers. It was one more quality that no doubt endeared her to George Augustus.

Henrietta's careful efforts to see off court drama are illustrated by her intervention in a petty scheme cooked up by Sophia Charlotte von Kielmansegg to cause trouble between the Princess of Wales and her ladies. Sophia Charlotte and Caroline of Ansbach were far from fond of one another and Sophia Charlotte also disliked Mary, Countess Cowper, who was friends with the princess. In 1714 Sophia Charlotte asked Lady Cowper to pass on a book to Caroline of Ansbach on her behalf. By employing the countess as a courier, the sly Sophia Charlotte knew full well that Caroline would assume that she and Lady Cowper were friends. That would be enough to make the princess cool on Lady Cowper. It really was the stuff of the playground.

Upon realising what Sophia Charlotte was up to, Henrietta advised Lady Cowper "that there was a mortal Hatred between [Sophia Charlotte and Caroline of Ansbach] and that the *Princess* thought her a wicked Woman." Henrietta warned Lady Cowper that Sophia Charlotte had specifically targeted her relationship with Caroline for "if it had not been so, she would have sent the book either by the Duchess of *Bolton* or Shrewsbury."[111] Though it certainly sounds petty to us, Lady Cowper learned a valuable lesson about court politics that day. Everybody was working an angle.

The young and accomplished maids of honour who surrounded the Princess of Wales became one of the central attractions of the court of George Augustus and his wife. They were celebrated for their sparkling personalities and could attract the most illustrious society names to their gatherings with a click of their fingers. Chief among their number was Charlotte Clayton, later Baroness Sundon, who was a particular favourite

---

111. Cowper, Mary (1865). *Diary of Mary Countess Cowper, Lady of the Bedchamber to the Princess of Wales, 1714 -1720.* London: John Murray, p.13.

of Caroline and who would, over the years of George II's reign, prove to be a thorn in the side of Robert Walpole himself. She and Henrietta were never destined to become close, but they had more in common than they might have guessed. Just as Henrietta would later be the person to whom people turned when seeking influence with George Augustus, Charlotte Clayton served the same role with Princess Caroline. Unlike Henrietta, Mrs Clayton relished her power.

George I and Melusine never courted the limelight. Instead they actively avoided it, living as private a life as they could in their rooms at St James's, but George Augustus couldn't have been more different. He and Caroline were the toast of the town and they loved it. They were sociable and cheery, and keen to prove themselves worthy of their adopted homeland. It made for a heady atmosphere among their attendants too, who found themselves at the centre of a glamorous court indeed.

Life in the household of the Prince and Princess of Wales was never dull whether they were dining in public, hosting a glittering ball, taking the air in the park, or simply basking in the love of their subjects. The public who viewed the dour George I with distrust lapped it up and grew ever fonder of his son and daughter-in-law, which irked the king no end. George I's coronation had been met with riots and protests and the threat from the Jacobites was a constant niggle. The last thing he needed was to be undermined by a son with whom relations were far from rosy, but things had already reached the point of no return. When George Louis appointed a regency council to rule in his absence during a trip to Hanover instead of entrusting his son with the job, the Prince of Wales felt the slight keenly. The stage was set for a fracture in the royal household.

The Split

With George I safely out of the picture in Hanover, Caroline and George Augustus embarked on a PR drive designed to win the hearts of their already adoring subjects. They knew how to play the popular card perfectly and declared at every opportunity in their heavy German accents that they considered themselves to be English through-and-through. George Augustus "thought [the English] the best, the handsomest, the best shaped, the best natured, and lovingest People in the World, and [if] Anybody would make their Court to him, it must be by telling him he was like an Englishman."[112] When measured against the sullen king, who maintained his Hanoverian habits and German language, George Augustus and Caroline were a breath of fresh air. Henrietta, meanwhile, continued to plough her own quiet furrow amongst the ladies of the court. Her decision to avoid politics had paid off and she could count friends across the factions that jostled for power around her, whilst her enemies appear to have been few. In fact, so celebrated was Henrietta's neutrality in court quarrels that she earned herself the nickname *the Swiss*, and her apartments became known as *the Swiss cantons*. It was a quality that would stand her in good stead for further advancement.

The woman whose life had once revolved around her son and a succession of filthy rooms now had a social circle to rival the very best. She welcomed the most celebrated characters of the Georgian era to her gatherings, including Dr John Arbuthnot, Alexander Pope and John Gay, who all became her firm friends. Where the most celebrated characters of the era went, George Augustus was sure to follow. Whether he was there for the company or to woo the lady remains to be seen.

George Augustus' fondness for Henrietta certainly hadn't gone unnoticed. Courtier Margaret Bradshaw even teased her about it in a

112. Ibid.

letter which reveals Henrietta's reputation as a favourite of the Prince of Wales, as well as paying homage to her late father.

"We have, said [Thomas Wharton, Marquis of Wharton], one lady, whom I can recommend to your friendship; her father was a son of the muses, and his daughter inherits her sire's wit; she is a great favourite of Pluto, and consequently of our Queen: all the Court are fond of her, she always being ready to do a good turn, and seldom speaks ill of any one."[113]

By the time George Louis arrived back from his visit to Hanover, tensions between him and George Augustus were greater than ever. When Caroline of Ansbach gave birth to a son in late 1717, what should have been a happy event instead lit the final touch paper. Things started badly when the king demanded that the infant be given the name George, a stipulation that the Prince and Princess of Wales agreed to despite their reservations. When George Louis then tried to impose Thomas Pelham-Holles, 1st Duke of Newcastle, as a godfather, however, the new parents put their foot down.

George Augustus and the duke had never got on and though the Prince of Wales was determined not to acquiesce to his father's demands, eventually the king won the day: the Duke of Newcastle would be George William's godfather. Emotions were still running high at the christening itself and after an altercation, Newcastle claimed that George Augustus had threatened his life. The king was apoplectic and demanded to know what exactly had occurred. George Augustus told him that he had told Newcastle, "you are a rascal, but I shall find you," meaning that he would show everyone that the duke was a thoroughly bad sort. Newcastle instead claimed that George Augustus had said, "I shall fight you!" and he was mortally offended. Even when the prince blamed the misunderstanding on his German accent the king wouldn't be swayed. He and the Prince of Wales had reached breaking point.

The idyllic summer Henrietta had spent hosting her gatherings was little more than a memory when she made her way to Caroline's rooms and was met by a shocking sight.

---

113. Margaret Bradshaw to Henrietta Howard, 21 August 1720, BL, Add. MS 22627, fol. 114.

"What was my astonishment [...] when going to the Princess's apartment the next morning, the yeomen in the guard-chamber pointed their halberds at my breast, and told me I must not pass! I urged that it was my duty to attend the Princess. They said, 'No matter I must not pass that way."[114]

Make no mistake, to find the way to the Princess of Wales barred by armed guards was no ordinary occurrence, but proof of the catastrophic rupture that had finally split the two halves of the family. It had begun decades earlier when George Louis had divorced his wife, George Augustus' mother, and allowed her to be imprisoned at Ahlden. She was not allowed to say goodbye to her children, nor to ever see them again, and they were forbidden from mentioning her in their father's earshot. Relations between George Louis and his son had never been particularly rosy from that day onwards, and things had become even more strained when the king insisted that Frederick must remain in Hanover when the rest of the royal party came to England. George Augustus was unable to visit Fred and didn't see him again for 14 years. When he did, they had become strangers.

George I was a regular visitor to Hanover throughout his reign and when he couldn't be there in person, he wrote long letters to his grandson. Through these letters and visits, George Augustus became convinced that his father was doing all he could to turn Fred against him. It was certainly no coincidence that when Melusine tried to influence the marriage plans of Fred and his sister, it was George I who held sway, not George Augustus. It's no coincidence either that when George Augustus succeeded to the throne, he wiped the marriage plans that his father had nurtured off the slate and hung a picture of his late mother in pride of place. George Louis lavished time and attention on Fred whilst simultaneously denying George Augustus and Caroline the right to see him. In doing so, he created a feud between father and son just like the one that had engulfed his own relationship with George Augustus. It was to become a destructive pattern for the men of the House of Hanover.

---

114. Walpole, Horace (1842). *Letters of Horace Walpole, Earl of Orford: Vol I*. London: Lea and Blanchard, p.83.

The outburst between George Augustus and the Duke of Newcastle at George William's christening was the final straw. The king banished the Prince of Wales from St James's Palace and Princess Caroline chose to leave with her husband. When she did, George Louis declared that the couple's children, including the newborn George William, would remain with him. Though Melusine did all she could to soothe the youngsters after the separation, it took a tragedy to soften George Louis' heart. When the infant George William fell mortally ill, George Louis grudgingly allowed the Prince and Princess of Wales to visit him at St James's Palace. It was a scant comfort, but even when three-month-old George William died, the king remained immovable. The royal households occupied different worlds.

George Augustus and Caroline established an alternative court at their new home of Leicester House, where they welcomed George I's political opponents in their droves. Robert Walpole was soon a regular visitor, for he had shrewdly identified that the supposedly unpolitical Caroline was anything but. Instead she was her husband's most trusted advisor and would prove to be as politically astute as she was influential. With George I already in his late fifties, Walpole was making sure that he held sway with the king's eventual successor too. He and Caroline would eventually form a strong bond that stood Walpole in excellent stead for the reign of George II.

The split between father and son inevitably had an impact on those who served them. The Howard family was still living at St James's Palace but with the removal of the Prince and Princess of Wales, that was set to change. Henrietta was expected to go to Leicester House with her mistress, Caroline, whilst Charles would remain at St James's to serve the king. Though Henrietta was glad for an excuse to escape her husband, she found the decision to do so surprisingly difficult. Being in the service of the monarch hadn't softened Charles and he was as cruel and disreputable as ever, but still Henrietta was morally conflicted. She wrestled with the vows she had taken when they married, unsure whether to finally leave her wayward husband. In the early years of her marriage she had tried to remain under the same roof as Charles wherever possible, enduring his abuse and derision and serving as little more than his slave, but even now the decision to flee wasn't one that she took easily. Nor was it a decision that would go unremarked by polite society.

As Henrietta tussled with the choice to either leave her husband and follow the princess, or to remain at the side of the man who had brutalised her, she was keenly aware of the implication it had for her future. She left behind a remarkable piece of writing in which she set down her thoughts on the matter and in which we can clearly see a woman in turmoil, who had been the victim of her husband's cruelty for far too long. It offers a rare and unfettered glimpse into Henrietta's head.

"What is ye Marriage vow? A Solemn Contract where two engage. The Woman promises Duty, affection, and Obedience to the mans commands; to Guard that Share of his Honour reposed in her Keeping. What is his part? To guide, to protect, to Support and Govern with mildness. Have I perform'd my part? In word and deed. How has [Charles Howard] answer'd his? In no one article. How Guided? To Evil; how protected or Suported me? Left distitute wanting ye common necessarys of life; not always from Misfortunes, but from Choice. What (from justice as well as from humanity nay even from his vows) ought to have been mine, employ'd to gratifie his passions. How Govern'd? With Tyranny; with Cruelty, my life in Danger. Then am not I free? All other Engagements cease to bind, if either contracting party's fail in their parts. Self presevation [sic] is the first law of Nature, are married Women then, the only part of human Nature that must not follow it? Are they expected to act upon higher Principles of Relegion and honour than any other part of the Creation? If they have Superiour Sense, Superiour fortitude and reason, then why a Salve to what's inferior to them? How vain, how trifling is my reasoning? Look round and see how few of my Sex are intyttled to govern, look on my self; consider myself and I shall soon perceive it is not that I am Superiour but as I reflect on one who is indeed inferiour to all Mankind. How dangerous is Power in Women's hands? Do I know so many Miserable Wives from Mans Tyranick Power as I know unhappy and rediculous Husband only made so by too much indulgence; nay do I know one Single instance where great tenderness if attended with Submision to a Womans will, is not unfortunate to the Husband either in his honour, his Quiet, or his fortune? Then own the power justly placed however I am the suffered. But still I must believe I am free.

What do I propose from this freedom? To hate the man I did before dispise. Wou'd I proclaim my missery, my shame? Wou'd I revenge my wrongs? The first gives pity or Contempt but no redress. The Second not in my power without involving my Self, his honour now is mine; had I none before I married? can I devide them? how loose his, and keep my own?"[115]

Whilst it's clear that Henrietta loathed her husband, *dispised* him, in her own words, there was nothing to be gained from making his failing public other than pity. Henrietta wanted none of that. She likewise dismissed revenge and focused instead on how best to extricate herself from a situation that had not been of her making. Throughout the marriage Charles had shown her nothing but cruelty and tyranny and in doing so, she wondered, had he not implicitly released her from the vows she had made as a young and hopeful bride? Henrietta considered those vows as solemn and binding as any legal contract and she had, over the years of misery and torment, endeavoured to fill her side of the agreement. Time and again she had acquiesced to Charles without question, letting him plunge them into debt, squander her money and drag her across the country under a pseudonym designed to escape their creditors. Charles, to the contrary, had broken every vow he had ever made to Henrietta and in doing so, she concluded that he had broken the contract that marriage had established between them. Morally, Henrietta determined that this freed her from her solemn oath, whatever polite society might say behind its hand.

Henrietta had made her choice. Against her husband's furious wishes, she packed her things and prepared to follow the Princess of Wales to Leicester House. It was the first time that Henrietta had expressly gone against Charles' wishes and he flew into a rage, mired in a delusion of self-pity as he told her that he had been far from a tyrant. In fact, he eventually convinced himself that his only fault had been his generosity, "making you so Independent on [sic] me"[116] that Henrietta had become wilful and allowed herself to be swept up in her new life with the princess.

---

115. Henrietta Howard, personal memorandum, 29 August 1716, BL, Add. MS 22627, fol. 13.
116. Charles Howard to Henrietta Howard, 22 February 1727/28, BL, Add. MS 22627, fol. 21.

Charles wanted his wife to give up her role in Caroline's retinue and, one suspects, fully expected that she would capitulate. She always had in the past, after all.

Instead, Henrietta stuck to her guns. Never before had she disobeyed her husband and it's likely that the certainty with which Henrietta clung to her plans rather wrongfooted him. Faced with losing his wife so publicly, Charles tried to save face by telling Henrietta that it didn't matter if she had decided to go or not, because instead he was now *ordering* her to leave his presence. As far as he was concerned, their marriage was over. It's entirely likely that the controlling Charles, who was not used to being told no, expected his dramatic grandstanding might win him the victory, but Henrietta had no love left for her husband. Instead he had given her precisely the escape route she needed. Charles Howard's furious tantrum served only to grant Henrietta her freedom. It would also cost her her son.

George I was happy to fan the flames of the dispute and blamed his son's caprice for splitting husband and wife. Charles Howard cared nothing for Henrietta beyond the cash he coerced from her, but he pursued her anyway, leaving Henrietta to accuse him of doing so in the "poor precarious expectation of court favours."[117] He didn't want her, she knew, all he wanted was to cosy up to the king. Henrietta, meanwhile, maintained her composure throughout, even going so far as to apologise to her brutal husband for speaking harshly to him when they parted. Yet by telling Henrietta that he considered her to have forfeited her position as his wife if she left, Charles played right into her hands. He had effectively confirmed what she had already decided: she was free to take whatever path she chose. Even Charles' threats to take legal action couldn't move Henrietta. By leaving, she pointed out, she had simply obeyed her husband when "[you] dismiss'd me from living any more with you"[118].

Though she was still not the king's mistress, leaving St James's Palace to remain with the Princess of Wales' household was as close to a respectable separation as Henrietta might hope to get. It provided her too with royal protection, a wage, and a roof over her head. The mutual contract of marriage that Henrietta had mused on in her private jottings had been well and truly severed.

---

117. Henrietta Howard to Charles Howard, 1727, BL, Add. MS 22627, fol. 24, 31.
118. Henrietta Howard to Charles Howard, c.1717, BL, Add. MS 22627, fol. 16.

Yet despite her introspection, Henrietta had reckoned without the depths of her husband's cruelty. In leaving St James's Palace she had humiliated Charles Howard and worse still, everyone in the gossip-fuelled hothouse of the royal court would know that she had gone. Furious and bent on revenge, he did the one thing that he knew without a doubt would hurt his wife more than any physical blow. Perhaps taking his lead from George I and his refusal to let his grandchildren go with their parents when they left the royal household, Charles did the same thing. He refused to let little Henry go to Leicester House with his mother and he forbade Henrietta from visiting her son again. The price of freedom had been high. Charles was determined that the son Henrietta adored would be taught to loathe her very name. He warned his wife that "No artifice, or Temptation of Reward upon earth, will ever Prevaile with him to desert me." As far as Charles was concerned, Henrietta had brought this last act of cruelty on herself and he would relish exacting his revenge. It was the one thing he did well.

Royal Favourite

Freed from the company of her husband and the drab confines of George I's court, Henrietta Howard flourished in her new life. She followed her own path just as Melusine had in Hanover, and she avoided intrigue and factionalism, instead remaining as neutral as possible. Henrietta, *the Swiss*, had perfected her poker face whilst enduring years of miserable married life, when an implacable public façade had been all she could cling onto. As those around Henrietta jostled for power, it was her steady calmness that made her an ideal member of Caroline's household. Not only was she trustworthy, well-bred and a perfectly proper society hostess, but she was also quick-witted and intelligent, two qualities that were highly valued amongst courtiers.

One man who noticed all of Henrietta's considerable qualities was George Augustus, the popular and sociable Prince of Wales. Given how indelibly she has since become associated with him, it might come as a surprise to learn that Henrietta wasn't at the top of George Augustus' wish list. That dubious honour belonged to her friend and fellow Woman of the Bedchamber, Mary Bellenden.

Mary was considered one of the great beauties of the court and Horace Walpole recorded "that I never heard her mentioned afterwards by one of her contemporaries who did not prefer her as the most perfect creature they ever knew"[119]. She was light-hearted and witty, and an ornament to Leicester House. She was also just the sort of woman that the Prince of Wales fancied for a mistress. But Mary Bellenden had other ideas. She had already fallen for her future husband, Colonel John Campbell, and she had no wish to miss out on the chance of happiness with him for the precarious role of the prince's mistress. But George Augustus was used to getting his own way and he had set his sights on Mary. For the money-

---

119. Walpole, Horace and Cunningham, Peter (ed.) (1877). *The Letters of Horace Walpole, Earl of Orford: Vol I*. London: Richard Bentley, p.124.

loving Prince of Wales, the obvious key to her seduction was his bank balance.

Horace Walpole mischievously recalled an evening when George Augustus took a seat beside Mary Bellenden, took out his purse and emptied it onto a table. Then, with great show and affectation, he began to loudly count out his money. Once he had finished counting, he repeated the show, each movement more pronounced than the last. If George Augustus thought this would be irresistible, he had badly misjudged Mary. After a little while she could stand it no longer and shrieked, "Sir, I cannot bear it: if you count your money any more, I will go out of the room!"[120] Despite her outburst, George Augustus displayed all the sensitivity customary of the gentlemen from Hanover and at a drawing room a few days later, the purse came out again. Blind to the absurdity of his actions, George Augustus went through the entire rigmarole all over again, emptying the coins and beginning to laboriously count each one in the presence of Mary Bellenden. This time Mary was more cunning and instead of asking him to stop, she *accidentally* knocked the piles of cash all over the floor. George Augustus, who was so miserly that he had once employed a page to lift up floorboards to find a single lost coin, quickly dropped to his knees to retrieve the scattered money and Mary used the diversion to escape. As Walpole wryly concluded, "the chink of the gold did not tempt her more than the person of his Royal Highness."[121]

George Augustus tried everything in his power to coax Mary into his arms, but she was set on Colonel Campbell. She took to displays of sullen disinterest whenever the prince was around and was so blatant that he took her to task for it. In a letter sent to Henrietta, Mary wrote that George Augustus asked her to tell a new lady-in-waiting that she should avoid certain behaviours, including "crossing her arms, as *I did to the Prince*, and [I] told him I was not cold, but I liked to stand so."[122] When all his efforts to seduce Mary failed, George Augustus became determined to discover who his rival for her affections was. The prince promised Mary that she and her love would both be favoured at court if they promised not to marry without first receiving his permission. Mary gave her word that

120. Ibid.
121. Ibid.
122. Ibid.

she wouldn't marry without letting George Augustus know, but refused to give him Campbell's name. When George Augustus learned that Mary had secretly married Campbell in 1720, he never forgave her. Every time he and Mary met after that, he reminded her sternly that she had broken her promise. George Augustus knew how to bear a grudge just as well as his father did.

With Mary Bellenden making her disinterest in the attentions of the Prince of Wales so unquestionably obvious, the field was clear for another candidate to try her luck. Henrietta's steady and calm manner had won her many friends and now George Augustus took to visiting her to pour out his heart, perhaps even to lament the loss of Mary Bellenden. He found Henrietta happy to provide a shoulder to cry on. She was already beginning to experience the fearsome headaches and hearing loss that would eventually leave her totally deaf, but she didn't let any of that dampen her pleasant nature. Pope, who adored Henrietta, was determined to turn her loss of hearing into something to be celebrated. He wrote:

> Has she no faults, then (Envy says), sir?
> Yes, she has one, I must aver:
> When all the world conspire to praise her,
> The *woman's deaf*, and will not hear."

Despite his determination to find a mistress, George Augustus remained devoted to his wife, Caroline, and she to him in a way that George I and Sophia Dorothea had never been. Yet royal mistresses were part of what kept the court wheels turning and Caroline accepted that it was simply the done thing, though she much preferred that her husband choose someone familiar to fill the role. With George Augustus acquiring a growing reputation as a man who was ruled by his forceful wife, he hoped that the presence of a mistress would serve as proof to court and parliament alike that he was in charge of his own affairs.

Exactly when and how George Augustus and Henrietta Howard became lovers remains open to conjecture. It seems unlikely that she set out to secure the role in a calculated manner, particularly given her earlier musings on the sanctity of her marriage vows, but neither should we see Henrietta as an innocent who was preyed upon by a lustful prince. It's more likely that the affair was born out of familiarity and friendship.

George Augustus liked to spend hours in Henrietta's quarters in the company of Mary and Henrietta, attempting to win Mary's affections whilst her friend played chaperone and third wheel. When Mary married and gave up her place at court in 1720, the meetings in Henrietta's rooms continued. This time, there were only two in attendance.

During the nightly audiences between Henrietta and George Augustus, who was six years her senior, the pair eventually came to an understanding. Horace Walpole famously did not "suppose that love had any share in the sacrifice she made of her virtue"[123] but rather imagined that Henrietta's capitulation came about because she "had felt poverty, and was far from disliking power."[124] Power, however, was something that would remain forever outside of her grasp. George Augustus had watched his father listen to the sometimes-errant advice of Melusine and had no wish for a mistress to become his advisor. That role belonged to his wife, Caroline of Ansbach.

Henrietta sought security rather than power after her unsettled childhood and poverty-stricken marriage. Her liaison with George Augustus provided security in spades, as well as a handsome allowance from her protector. She received £2,000 per year when he was prince, and this soared to an eyewatering £3,200 once he became king. That she achieved all this without incurring enemies and "from the propriety and decency of her behaviour was always treated as if her virtue had never been questioned,"[125] is testament to Henrietta's easy nature as she presided over the so-called Swiss cantons. Even after she retired, Henrietta continued to bank a pension of £2,000 per annum until George II died. Not that Henrietta shirked from performing that favourite pastime of the royal mistress – acquiring favours. It should come as no surprise that her brother, John, steadily climbed the ranks at court once she became George Augustus' mistress[126]. He would remain one of her closest friends.

Jonathan Swift, who had so savagely skewered Melusine when he had branded her a whore in his *A Wicked Treasonable Libel*, was a little kinder to Henrietta than to her fellow royal mistress. She was above all things a

123. Ibid., pp.CXXV.
124. Ibid.
125. Ibid., pp.CXXVII–CXXVIII.
126. Hobart followed the family tradition and entered politics in 1715. He became Treasurer of the Chamber in 1727 and Baron Hobart in 1728. In 1746 he was created 1st Earl of Buckinghamshire.

courtier, he decided, wielding the word like a weapon. To be a consummate courtier was far from a good thing, and Swift was sure that none was better at the game than Henrietta Howard.

"From the attendance duly paid her by all the ministers," Swift wrote, "as well as others who expect advancement, she hath been reckoned for some years to be the great favourite of the court at Leicester-fields, which is a fact that of all others she most earnestly wishes might not be believed."[127] It wasn't that Henrietta attempted to hide her position as favourite though, more that it wasn't in her retiring nature to capitalise on it as richly as others might have been tempted to do. Yet even Swift couldn't bring himself to level his sights at Henrietta as mercilessly as he had Melusine. "In all offices of life, except that of a courtier," he allowed, "she acts with justice, generosity, and truth; she is ready to do good as a private person [and] she will not do hurt as a courtier, unless it be to those who deserve it."[128]

For many years Swift adored Henrietta despite his criticisms and they exchanged regular letters, sharing stories and jokes and just a hint of affection. Theirs was certainly no love affair, but they were well-matched intellectually. He teased her endlessly, revelling in her attention and that of her mistress, both of whom were immeasurably fond of him. When Swift claimed that "there is no politician who [...] can form a language with more imperceptible dexterity to the present situation of the court, or more early foresee what style may be proper upon any approaching juncture of affairs, whereof she can gather timely intelligence without asking it, and often when those from whom she receives it do not know that they are giving it to her,"[129] however, he was mistaken. Henrietta was far from a gifted politician. In that regard, she was certainly inferior to the Princess of Wales.

Quite apart from influence and advancement, Henrietta had been glad of the opportunity that the Prince and Princess of Wales' departure from St James's Palace had given her to escape. She had the protection of royal favour and if she was to become the mistress of George Augustus, then that protection would become virtually ironclad. In this, she and Melusine

---

127. Howard, Henrietta, Countess of Suffolk (1824). *Letters to and from Henrietta, Countess of Suffolk, Vol I.* London: John Murray, p.xxxix.
128. Ibid., p.xli.
129. Ibid., p.xxxix.

were not so different. Both had joined the royal court as a means of finding a place to settle after precarious early years during which they had been forced to grow up quickly. As mistresses to a king and his heir respectively, they would finally achieve something approaching security. Though there's little doubt in my mind that Melusine and George I did love one another, how much love existed between Henrietta and George Augustus is a matter of debate. Royal marriages and royal mistresses shared one thing in common: they were often a matter of business before pleasure. Likewise, we should be careful not to view their attachment through the moral prism of Henrietta cuckolding her employer, Caroline of Ansbach, with George Augustus. In fact, the Princess of Wales far preferred that George Augustus take a mistress who she not only knew well, but actually had authority over. Years later, when George Augustus tired of Henrietta and sought a younger candidate who wasn't from within Caroline's inner circle, she was unsettled. By then a queen, Caroline became determined to ensure that Henrietta retained her position as George Augustus' *maîtresse-en-titre* against everyone's better wishes.

The waspish and spiky Baron Hervey, who Henrietta certainly couldn't count among her champions, lamented what he saw as an ill-matched couple. Indeed, he might almost have been speaking of Charles Howard too when he wrote of Henrietta and George Augustus:

> "She was civil to everybody, friendly to many, and unjust to none: in short, she had a good head and a good heart, but had to do with a man who was incapable of tasting the one or valuing the other."[130]

The liaison between George Augustus and Henrietta does not seem to have been the most passionate, it must be said. The prince made his nightly visits to her chambers just as his father did to Melusine's rooms, and there he and Henrietta passed a few hours in private. He would arrive at her door every evening on the dot of nine and was so slavishly devoted to routine that he paced his own rooms until the very minute of their meeting arrived. He was keen to see her, but not so keen that he didn't stick rigidly to his timetable.

---

130. Croker, John Wilson (ed.) (1848). *Memoirs of the Reign of George II from his Accession to the Death of Queen Caroline by John, Lord Hervey: Vol I*. London: John Murray, p.96.

Though there have been historical accounts that claim the relationship between the prince and Henrietta was never more than platonic, few today would agree with that supposition. George Augustus wasn't the most cerebral man in the world but was instead hot-tempered and had a penchant for tantrums, kicking his wigs and stamping his feet when things didn't go his way. He loved the company of women, none more so than his wife, and there were plenty of young ladies at court who would have happily shared his bed. To think that he spent a few hours each evening discussing matters of note with Henrietta is simply not plausible. He preferred to do *that* with his wife.

Henrietta was not a showy mistress. Instead she downplayed her position, remaining as neutral and self-contained as ever. Yet the fact that she had the ear of the heir to the throne could not go unnoticed. Soon, "the busy and speculative politicians of the anti-chambers [sic], who know everything, but know everything wrong, naturally concluded, that a lady with whom the King passed so many hours every day must necessarily have some interest with him, and consequently applied to her"[131].

Caroline had allied herself with Robert Walpole, who she had come to trust after he had engineered the reconciliation between her husband and his father. Walpole's opponents knew they had no hope of influence with the Princess of Wales, so they made the prince's mistress their target instead. It was a wasted effort for the most part and when George Augustus succeeded to the throne, poems and ballads mocked his reliance on his shrewd and politically intelligent wife with verses that savaged the monarch and his family.

"You may strut, dapper George, but 'twill all be in vain;
We all know 'tis Queen Caroline, not you, that reign –
You govern no more than Don Philip of Spain.
Then if you would have us fall down and adore you,
Lock up your fat spouse, as your dad did before you."

---

131. Mahon, Lord (ed.) (1845). *The Letters of Philip Dormer Stanhope, Earl of Chesterfield: Vol II*. London: Richard Bentley, p.441.

There was a good portion of truth in the jesting. Robert Walpole spotted early on that advancement and favour lay in the hands not of the mistress, but of the wife. For that wife, meanwhile, power became the bluntest instrument she possessed.

Royal Servant

As a Woman of the Bedchamber, Henrietta Howard was ostensibly the lady whose job it was to help the Princess of Wales with her toilette routine. For years Henrietta had carried out her duties without complaint but now that her servant was sharing her favours with George Augustus, Caroline's love of protocol went into overdrive. She tightened Henrietta's leash.

Perhaps the one incident that demonstrates more than ever the uncomfortable dichotomy of Henrietta's dual roles comes in a story that Baron Hervey related of a clash between wife and mistress. By rights, Henrietta was required to hold the basin from which Caroline washed each morning, and she was supposed to kneel whilst doing so. Though this might not seem like the most arduous of tasks, the queen's washing regime wasn't exactly quick, nor was it particularly ceremonial. Instead, Henrietta knelt with the basin in her hands as Caroline washed wherever she felt needed cleaning, including picking out her teeth and flicking the detritus into the basin that Henrietta held. So much for royal glamour.

Caroline, who had been so friendly for so long towards her servant, suddenly and quite unexpectedly decided that every ceremony must now be followed to the letter. Sensing that her mistress' change of behaviour was dictated not by protocol but by jealousy, Henrietta allowed herself a rare moment of rebellion. To Caroline, who shared the story with Baron Hervey, it was simply a source of spiteful amusement. Henrietta could rebel all she liked, but ultimately, both knew that she was powerless.

"[Henrietta dared] to pick a quarrel with me about holding a basin in the ceremony of my dressing, and to tell me, with her little fierce eyes, and cheeks as red as your coat, that positively she would not do it; to which I made her no answer then in anger, but calmly, as I would have said to a naughty child, "Yes, my dear Howard, I am sure you will; indeed you will. Go, go! Fa for shame! Go, my good Howard; we will talk of this another time."

About a week after, when upon maturer deliberation she had done everything about the basin that I would have her, I told her I knew we should be good friends again; but could not help adding, in a little more serious voice, that I owned of all my servants I had least expected, as I had least deserved it, such treatment from her, when she knew I had held her up at a time when it was in my power, if I had pleased, any hour of the day, to let her drop through my fingers thus."[132]

And so it was to continue for Henrietta, who could do nothing but take her mistreatment on the chin unless she wanted to run the risk of being thrown out of her job. She couldn't expect anything in the way of support from George Augustus either. Were he ever to be called upon to decide between his wife and his mistress, there was only one way he would jump. Horace Walpole recalled that after George Augustus' succession to the throne, he and Caroline continued to use Henrietta in a humiliating manner, upbraiding her for being jealous and threatening her with the sack if she dared to answer back. George Augustus was no courtly lover, and he was not above turning on his mistress to impress his wife either. On one occasion as Henrietta was dressing the queen, George Augustus burst into the room and snatched a kerchief from Caroline's neck. He rounded furiously on Henrietta and bellowed, "Because you have an ugly neck yourself, you love to hide the Queen's!". How that barb must have stung.

George Augustus was entirely reliant on Caroline in many matters and sought absolution from his extramarital conquests by making sure that they received the approval of his wife. Whenever George Augustus fell for a woman, he made sure to tell Caroline all about her in the most elaborate and lurid detail. His letters ran to dozens of pages and described in painstaking detail the woman he was pursuing. He catalogued her best and worst qualities and culminated in a detailed commentary on the

---

132. Croker, John Wilson (ed.) (1848). *Memoirs of the Reign of George II from his Accession to the Death of Queen Caroline by John, Lord Hervey: Vol II.* London: John Murray, pp.16–17.

seduction itself. Caroline was his closest advisor in all things, not just matters of national importance.

Though Caroline likely never gave any serious consideration to terminating Henrietta's appointment, there was always the possibility that she *could* and that would spell certain catastrophe for Henrietta. Her place at Leicester House protected her from her brutal husband but that place was dependent on remaining in good favour. Of course, it helped that she had been so *Swiss* in her manner, acquiring few if any enemies along the way, and it helped too that she was never showy in her relationship with George Augustus. If anything, by her quiet nature Henrietta did all she could to ensure that the affair remained as private as was possible in the Georgian court. Even then Caroline liked to occasionally tighten the screws, just to remind her servant who was the boss. Whenever she felt as though Henrietta was getting too popular, either with Walpole's enemies or George Augustus himself, she would concoct political business to keep her husband busy and away from his mistress. By these small means, she kept her rival in check.

In fact, Caroline really had no need to keep Henrietta in check, because Henrietta was singularly unsuccessful when it came to the political side of her role. Melusine had sold favours and titles to the highest bidder as a matter of routine and had, through some shrewd whispers in the king's ears, advanced her favourites and kept her enemies mostly at bay. There is considerably less proof of Henrietta having done anything on the same scale. Instead she was a royal mistress in the most basic sense, spending hour after hour with the prince, who could be as sullen and bad-tempered as his father was, always at his beck and call just as she was at that of the princess. Through all of it she must have told herself that it was worth the stultifying boredom of George Augustus' company to be safe from her husband, but being safe from Charles brought with it separation from her son too.

Henrietta could only imagine what Charles had been telling Henry in the years since she had last seen him, but I think we can guess. He had resolved to make the boy hate his mother and, in becoming mistress to the Prince of Wales, Henrietta had provided her estranged spouse with ample ammunition. No doubt to the impressionable boy she was the scarlet woman, abandoning her child to cosy up to the heir to the throne and reap all the rewards that her new role would bring with it. Henrietta mourned the loss of Henry, so to see the royal couple separated from their children after the move to Leicester House must have brought back miserable memories.

Because of her estrangement from her own son, there were some amongst Henrietta's circle who believed that she must have had some hand in the reconciliation between the king and the prince. Elizabeth Molesworth, Henrietta's friend and correspondent, wrote that "I suppose you have had no small share in the joy this happy reconciliation has occasioned", but in fact Henrietta gained little from it.

Perhaps Henrietta had hoped that the reconciliation of the prince and his father might bring with it the occasional opportunity to visit St James's Palace and catch the odd glimpse of her son, but it was not to be. When Caroline's pleas to Robert Walpole and Melusine finally brought about the uneasy peace, it was far from happy families. Though the public rejoiced at the apparent reunion between the royal father and son, in truth it was more of a PR exercise than any real meeting of the minds and the mutual animosity between the king and the prince certainly hadn't been resolved, only papered over. The courts remained two separate entities, though courtiers could now pass more freely between them, even if the households didn't come together as one. At drawing rooms and other events, the king and his entourage occupied one side of the room whilst the prince and his circle stuck to the other. There was little true unity. George Augustus remained at Leicester House and summered at Richmond Lodge and so did Henrietta, her son lost to her still. That was one thing that wouldn't change.

New Horizons

It was now five years since Henrietta had seen her son. Freedom from Charles had come at a dreadful price, but she contented herself with piecing together Henry's life from what little information her friends were able to glean. He had been sent away to school, she learned, and perhaps she hoped that the distance this would put between father and son might go in her favour. Left alone to discover his own mind, there was always the faint hope that young Henry might resolve to seek out his mother of his own accord. Sadly, that was something Henry Howard never did.

At Leicester House the circle that had once contained Henrietta's friends was shrinking as marriage carried the other maids of honour away. She was more aware than ever that many of those politicians who now sought to win her friendship did so with one eye on their future ambitions. Just as the king's political opponents were regular callers at the Prince of Wales' court, so too did that same court inevitably divide into factions, with Walpole and Caroline on one side and Henrietta and Walpole's enemies on the other. It was not what Henrietta, who had created a home for herself in the *Swiss cantons*, had envisioned for herself. The relationship between Melusine and George I was more like that of a married couple, but that of Henrietta and George Augustus was never so close. She would always be second to his beloved Caroline of Ansbach, no matter how much influence ambitious politicians might think she wielded.

The role of mistress to a bad-tempered, grumpy heir to the throne who wanted nothing more than to see the back of his father was not one to be relished. Henrietta's friends certainly knew of her growing dissatisfaction with her place. As early as 1720 Mary Bellenden, by now Mary Campbell, wrote to Henrietta to commiserate with her on her situation. It is significant that in signing off, she wrote, "My dear Howard, God bless you, and send health *and liberty*. Don't show this, I charge you, at your peril."[133] Liberty was definitely on Henrietta's mind and she had begun

---

133. Mary Campbell to Henrietta Howard, 1720, BL, Add. MS 22627, fol. 89.

saving once again. Though she had sold everything from her jewels to her bed linen first to pay the rent then to fund the trip to Hanover, her role as the Prince of Wales' mistress made the matter of building a nest egg considerably easier.

As the years passed and Henrietta and George Augustus grew more distant, her financial acumen would prove to be invaluable. By the time Mary informed Henrietta that there was already court gossip suggesting that things had soured between the prince and his mistress, that same mistress was already plotting her escape. Each letter from the women who had once been Henrietta's contemporaries at court brought new tales of happy marriages and fashionable trips to take the waters or to dance the night away, but all of that was denied to Henrietta. Perhaps luckily for her though, just as she was looking for a way to escape the court, so too was George Augustus; bored by his mistress and seeking new entertainment, he was equally keen to send her packing.

Aware of the need to ensure his mistress' future if he hoped to one day be rid of her, George Augustus offered Henrietta a settlement of £11,500, a significant proportion of which was made up of shares in the infamous South Sea Company. That money, along with other gifts, provided Henrietta with a sum that was entirely safe from the grasping hands of her estranged husband, and offered her the very real chance of starting a new life away from the royal court. Caroline of Ansbach, however, had other plans. Henrietta Howard was a known figure, a case of better the devil you know than the devil you don't. She was Caroline's servant and had long since been taught to know her place. The Princess of Wales wasn't about to let her husband trade Henrietta in for a potentially more threatening replacement without putting up a fight.

Caroline didn't interfere in Henrietta's schemes for now, but instead allowed her to go about quietly making plans for a life beyond the court. In order to keep her plans private, Henrietta retained the services of her friend the Earl of Ilay, who she engaged to purchase land in Twickenham on her behalf. It was there that she would eventually construct her sanctuary of Marble Hill House. Henrietta continued adding to this initial parcel of land over the next few years, gradually increasing her estate a little bit at a time in the hope that Charles wouldn't notice. By this point, Twickenham was a fashionable place for those who wanted to escape the hustle and bustle of London. It was also close to the royal summer residence of Richmond Lodge, which George Augustus had taken possession of in 1719, and a country residence in Twickenham was a sure sign that a Georgian had really made it. It was here that Henrietta, increasingly plagued by deafness, envisioned herself living out the rest of her days, far from court intrigues and her grumpy lover and his watchful wife. The house itself was designed by architect Roger Morris and Lord Pembroke, and by the summer of 1723, a plan of her dream home was all but completed.

With Charles alert to any developments in his wife's situation, secrecy was of paramount importance, but still Henrietta shared news of the project with a small and trusted circle. Amongst that circle were Pope, Gay and Lords Bathurst, Peterborough, and Burlington, all of whom played their part in bringing Henrietta's cherished plans to fruition and oversaw construction of her new home on her behalf. When the Prince and Princess of Wales acquired Richmond Lodge, Caroline had employed Pope to help her improve the grounds and in the gardens and fanciful grottos of Marble Hill, which looked out over the Thames, he would demonstrate his exceptional skills once more. It was a worrying show of independence for a royal mistress.

True to form for a woman who had navigated the choppy waters of court without making many enemies, once the work at Twickenham became widely known, Henrietta's friends and admirers flocked to lend a hand wherever it might be needed.

Henrietta had always been popular at court on account of her good nature and ready access to the prince, but among her friends and confidantes were some who were a little more keen on her than others. Two came to the fore in the shape of Earl Bathurst and the Earl of Peterborough, and that was enough to irritate the Prince of Wales. Ironically, their interest was all it took to effectively scupper Henrietta's chances of getting away. Just as she had once been in thrall to Charles, now it was the heir to the throne who was effectively deciding Henrietta's future for her.

Charles Mordaunt, 3rd Earl of Peterborough, was 65 years old when he set his cap at Henrietta. His life had been one of adventure, marked by the highest highs and lowest lows, not least of which was a spell in the Tower of London for his suspected role in a Jacobite conspiracy. Mordaunt had made a comeback during the reign of Queen Anne, when he had returned to his political career and saw active military service. Fiery, something of a romantic and with an eye for the ladies, this ageing Casanova had secretly married opera singer Anastasia Robinson in 1722 but, even with a wife more than 30 years his junior, he couldn't help but fall for Henrietta. Lady Hervey, formerly known as Melusine's rival Molly Lepell, sent Henrietta an amusing note which perhaps summed up the unusual character of Mordaunt perfectly.

> "[Lord Mordaunt] wear boots all day, and, as I hear, must do so, having brought no shoes with him, and a cabbage under each arm, or a chicken in his hand, which, after he himself has purchased at market, he carries home for his dinner."[134]

Yet Lord Mordaunt, earthy and temperamental, could be a poet too. He wrote a ballad in praise of Henrietta which was filled with exultations to her wit and beauty, singing the praises of the almost otherworldly woman who had captured his heart. The ballad concludes with the following stanza:

> O wonderful creation! A woman of reason!
> Never grave out of pride, never gay out of season;
> When so easy to guess who this angel should be,
> Would one think Mrs. Howard ne'er dreamt it was she?

The earl penned long and loving letters to Henrietta but they weren't necessarily indicative of sexual intimacy between the two of them. Rather they were old fashioned, courtly love letters, filled with breathless flights of fancy and adoring promises. They're certainly not what one would expect from an old soldier in his sixties who'd already had his fair share of romantic adventures. Peterborough, one might say, had got it bad.

"As I can as well live without meat and sleep as without thinking of her who had possession of my soul," he wrote to Henrietta, "so to find some relief, in never having any conversation with this adored lady, I have been forced, when alone, to make many and many a dialogue betwixt her and myself."[135] In his letters he reproached Henrietta for not replying

---

134. Lady Hervey to Henrietta Howard, 7 June 1725, BL, Add. MS 22628, fol. 13.
135. The Earl of Peterborough to Henrietta Howard, c.1723, BL, Add. MS 22625, fol. 40.

with similar declarations of love, but how on earth could she? Even if she shared his feelings, and there's absolutely no proof that she did, Henrietta's place at court was still precarious even after all these years. Should George Augustus withdraw his favours, the future wouldn't necessarily be bright.

Unsure of how to proceed, Henrietta enlisted the help of her friend, John Gay, to construct a response to Peterborough. How far his assistance went we can't be sure, but as Peterborough's flowery letters continued Henrietta answered them not as a lover, but as a thinker. She questioned her would-be suitor more closely about how he saw the nature of love and particularly how he regarded the role of the woman in the pursuit that he seemed so intent on undertaking. What emerges most of all from her replies is a very gentle, yet rather firm rejection. Henrietta wanted to discuss logic, not emotion.

> "Every one that loves think his own mistress an Amoret; and, therefore, ask any lover who and what Amoret is, he will describe his own mistress as she appears to himself; but the common practice of men of gallantry is, to make an Amoret of every lady they write to. And, my lord, after you have summed up all the fine qualities that are necessary to make an Amoret, I am under some apprehensions you will conclude with a compliment by saying I am she."[136]

The more decorous and romantic Peterborough's letters became, the more logical were Henrietta's replies. She deconstructed his melodramatic talk of dying for the want of love or exiling himself if she rejected him, and pointed out instead that he had been a soldier in his day, a man who had faced very real dangers and survived them. He would survive this too, she assured him. Perhaps in a lastditch effort to win his adored Henrietta to his arms, Lord Peterborough sent her the ballad he had composed in her honour. In fact, as far as Henrietta was concerned this sealed the deal. She thanked him politely for his interest but informed her admirer that his ballad merely provided a perfect example of "the ridiculous cant of love."[137] True love wasn't expressed in high blown words and lyrical ballads, she admonished Peterborough, but in the slightest glance or hushed word. One shouldn't have to *think* about love, it should come naturally.

---

136. Henrietta Howard to the Earl of Peterborough, c.1723, BL, Add. MS 22625, fol. 54.
137. Henrietta Howard to the Earl of Peterborough, c.1723, BL, Add. MS 22625, fol. 82.

Lord Peterborough took it on the chin. He continued to adore Henrietta from afar whilst consoling himself with the charms of his secret bride, but there were those among the courtiers who were convinced that things had progressed further than the simple exchange of letters. Idle gossip, no doubt, and certainly not borne out at all by the content of Henrietta's replies. There was always a certain element of flirtation between courtiers. For example, Henrietta liked to write to Lord Chesterfield in the guise of her little dog, Marquise, and he would reply as though addressing the canine directly. Decades later when both were elderly, she and Chesterfield corresponded playfully again, this time in the guise of a maid in Henrietta's household and a footman in Chesterfield's. There was never a romance, merely a shared love of silliness and a bit of starry-eyed flirtation, or *frizelation*, as Henrietta termed it.

Idle gossip attached itself too to Allan Bathurst, 1st Earl Bathurst, who shared Peterborough's longing to win Henrietta's love. Only five years divided Henrietta and Earl Bathurst in age and, like so many members of her own family, he had pursued a political career. A close friend of Alexander Pope's and a political opponent of Robert Walpole, Bathurst was a natural fit for Henrietta's particular circle. He was also married, but that wasn't really an obstacle to anything at the Georgian court.

Bathurst and Henrietta became far firmer friends than she and Peterborough ever were, and he was invaluable in the construction of Marble Hill. He and Pope drew up plans for the grounds in concert with Henrietta, and the closer they worked, the more the gossip swirled at Leicester House. Whether the friendship went beyond that of a *frizelation* is debateable, but I suspect not. Henrietta's position at court was worth more to her than rumpled bedsheets and the odd night of passion. Then, quite suddenly and just as quickly as the gossip had started, it stopped. Lady Mary Wortley Montagu, who had done her bit to fan the flames by spreading rumours of the earl and Henrietta, was sure that George Augustus had had words with his mistress and warned her that enough was enough. "The fair lady," wrote Lady Mary, "[was] given to understand by her commanding officer, that if she shewed [sic] under other colours, she must expect to have her pay retrenched."[138] That was all it took to dampen the rumoured amour between the earl and the lady.

---

138. Wortley Montagu, Lady Mary (1837). *The Letters and Works of Lady Mary Wortley Montagu, Vol I*. London: R Bentley, pp.164–165.

As the building at Marble Hill progressed, Henrietta was still stuck at court with the jealous Prince of Wales, and though he certainly didn't really want her for himself anymore, he equally didn't want anyone else to have her instead. Kept busy with the stultifying duties of the household, she could only listen in rapt excitement as her friends told her of how well work on the villa was progressing. As Marble Hill took shape they dined there and toasted their absent friend, but Henrietta at least knew that her cherished sanctuary was being cared for. For now, she could still only dream of closing her own front door.

Marital Strife

It likely came as no surprise to Henrietta that, when news spread of her purchase of land in Twickenham and the subsequent construction of Marble Hill, her husband reared his head once more. Charles had continued to be a thorn in his estranged wife's side from afar, lobbying her trustees for money at the same time as going into battle with his own brother, now the 8th Earl of Suffolk. The conflict had come about when the 7th Earl, their nephew, died without an heir in 1722. He left a will that bequeathed Audley End to Charles, whilst Edward succeeded to the title. Edward was outraged at this perceived slight and took Charles to court to claim ownership of the family estate. He failed, but an agreement was reached whereby Charles must pay Edward a nominal sum each year from the estate. Naturally, Charles didn't give his brother a penny. How could he, when he was still the dissolute soak he had always been?

When Edward came calling to collect his money, Charles fell back on his old ways and turned to Henrietta. As a member of George I's entourage, he naturally knew all about the payment of £11,500 that she had received from George Augustus. When he then saw the beautiful home that his wife was having built at Twickenham, he became convinced that he deserved a share of her good fortune. This time Charles took a different approach. Rather than relying on intimidation, he pretended instead that he was repentant and longed only to be reunited with his estranged wife. Henrietta certainly had no wish to be forced back into her husband's society after so many years apart, but Charles wasn't about to go away. Instead he wrote to the Princess of Wales in the guise of the wounded party. In his letter he assured Caroline that it wasn't merely *his* wish that Henrietta be relieved of her duties, but the king's royal command.

"It is with the greatest respect and Deference, that I presume Addressing myself to your Royal Highnesse in this manner. When I first received the King's commands for my wife to leave your

Royal Highnesse's Service, the persuasions I used with her were innefectual and this morning I have again received his positive directions, that she immediately retires from her Employment under your Royal Highnesse. I cannot be insensible of my unhappiness in this difficulty, which makes me hope Your Royal Highnesse will not impute it as any disrespect in me recalling of her by the King's Commands being unavoidable for me to disobey."[139]

Caroline showed the letter to Henrietta to gauge her response. She probably derived some pleasure in doing so too, because it allowed her to remind her Woman of the Bedchamber that all it would take was a word from the royal household and she'd be returned to her abusive spouse. Yet even if the princess did feel a little satisfaction in this obvious demonstration of power, Henrietta probably knew that she would remain protected in her role. After all, Caroline still held true to her *better the mistress you know* opinion. When Henrietta rejected her husband's advances, Charles went for broke and pulled out what he must have expected to be the biggest gun of all. If she wouldn't come home for him, he said, then perhaps she would for her child.

"I can say no more to persuade you," he wrote, "(if you have any thought of ease to the small posterity of a child you seemed to love) how ungrateful and shocking a part he must share in life, to hear the reproaches of your public defiance to me, and what the world will interpret the occasion of it." In refusing to return to him, said Charles, Henrietta was shaming her son all over again. It was a calculated twist of the knife. He closed his letter with the self-pitying cry of the supposedly wronged spouse, signing off as "a man who always loved you, and will continue doing it"[140]. There was no truth in that whatsoever.

To make sure his scheme met with success, Charles petitioned the Archbishop of Canterbury, Dr William Wake, to ask the Princess of Wales whether she would be willing to intervene. The archbishop explained in his letter to Caroline that Charles was on the verge of obtaining a writ that would force Henrietta to leave the royal service. The delivery of this writ

---

139. Charles Howard to the Princess of Wales, 21 April 1727, BL, Add. MS 22627, fol. 27.
140. Charles Howard to Henrietta Howard, 2 May 1727, BL, Add. MS 22627, fol. 30.

to Leicester House would be a source of some public embarrassment, Dr Wake warned, and he urged Caroline to act now to avoid being dragged into the messy proceedings. Things between the two Georges were hardly rosy after all.

The Archbishop of Canterbury, however, had reckoned without Caroline's love of the status quo. Henrietta was her woman and more importantly, she was a tame mistress to the Prince of Wales. The princess had no intention of upsetting that well-established arrangement. This time when Henrietta responded to her husband, it was in the sure knowledge that the Princess of Wales would not cave in to Charles Howard's demands, even if the king had made a royal command of them. She reminded Charles that he had ordered her out of his house and even invoking the name of their son would not see her return.

"[After] having been directly dismissed by you and absolutely discharged your company, after your passions having led you to say more of me than I can with decency repeat, what refuge more safe, more honourable or more rational can a wife so abandoned by her husband have recourse to than to continue in the service of the Princess of Wales where to her husband's great satisfaction and to his and her own honour she was formerly placed?

You mention, Sir, a tender subject indeed, my child. I wish to God he was of a riper age to be a judge between us; I cannot but flatter myself he would have more duty and humanity than to desire to see his mother exposed to misery and want if not by his father's commands, by yet worse by the influence men in power have over him."[141]

When his efforts met with rejection, Charles' threats to resort to legal action became a reality. He obtained a warrant from the Lord Chief Justice that he claimed gave him the absolute right to seize his wife by force if that was the only means necessary. Henrietta was terrified and made a prisoner of herself at Leicester House as surely as George I had made a prisoner of his wife at Ahlden. Charles might be impetuous in his anger, but even he knew better than to mount an assault on a royal household, so

---

141. Henrietta Howard to Charles Howard, 2 May 1727, BL, Add. MS 22627, fol. 28.

for now she was safe. If she left the confines of Leicester House though, the danger could become very real indeed. Horace Walpole, a friend and neighbour of Henrietta's in her later life, related an eyebrow-raising story that perfectly illustrated just how afraid Henrietta really was of her husband.

As the summer of 1727 approached, the Prince of Wales and his household prepared for their usual jaunt to their summer home at Richmond Lodge. Naturally Henrietta was expected to go too, but she was convinced that Charles would attempt to seize her on the road. Eventually a plan was concocted whereby Henrietta's friends, the Duke of Argyll and the Earl of Ilay, would spirit her away at dawn and get her safely out of London hours before the royal party left for Richmond. Though Henrietta made the journey safely she had no more freedom in Richmond than she had in London. Instead she spent the summer hidden away from the clutches of Charles Howard. It was a miserable time.

Henrietta knew that something had to change and if Charles had obtained a writ, then legal measures were all that remained for her too. With that in mind, she approached lawyer James Welwood and asked him to negotiate with Charles on the terms of a formal separation.

Mistress to a King

As Henrietta and James Welwood waited to see if Charles would consent to a separation, and if so what his no doubt exorbitant terms would be, a veritable earthquake rattled the royal court. During his trip home to Hanover in June 1727, King George I had died. With that, the son he'd never got on with succeeded to the throne. George Augustus and his party were still at Richmond Lodge when news of the king's death reached them, but they packed up with all haste and made for London. Any hopes Henrietta might have entertained of finally moving into her Marble Hill sanctuary were dashed by the succession and she would have been all too aware of that fact. A king needed a mistress and that mistress was Henrietta Howard. Of course, this king's mistress was also a servant, and that meant that she had a queen to kowtow to. When George Augustus was crowned, Henrietta was there to tend to Caroline in a gown of scarlet and silver with lavish trimming, her hair dressed with silver ribbon. She was still a servant above all else.

> "Mrs. Howard and Mrs. Neale, two of her Majesty's Bed-Chamber Women, are to walk in the Procession at the approaching Coronation."[142]

If Henrietta's company had been in demand among ambitious courtiers at Leicester House, once the new king and his household repaired to the city, she found herself more popular than ever. Everybody wanted an audience with the king's mistress, whose nightly meetings with the new monarch made her the hottest of properties. Unlike Melusine, Henrietta wasn't so keen to sell titles and favours to the highest bidder and instead of glorying in her newfound power, the increased stress began to tell upon her as her headaches grew worse. When she did try to influence George

---

142. *Daily Journal*. 20 September 1727; issue 2086.

II on behalf of her friends, Caroline was quick to smack Henrietta down, reminding her time and again that there was only one queen at the court of St James's.

Never was Henrietta's lack of power more obvious that in the unfortunate case of her friends, John Gay and Jonathan Swift. Henrietta was immensely fond of Gay, a long-serving courtier who had so far received no official recognition for his loyalty, and she asked George Augustus if he could find a paid role for him in the household. George Augustus, we might assume, discussed the matter with Caroline and Gay was duly offered the far from glamorous and very poorly paid position of Gentleman Usher to the infant Princess Louisa. Gay and Henrietta were both stung by this veiled insult, and he gave up his attendance at court, recognising now that there was to be no special favour for him.

Swift had always been a rather more acerbic friend of Henrietta's and when he saw his own hopes of advancement dashed too, he reacted bitterly. Though Gay held no personal resentment towards Henrietta, Swift laid the blame for his disappointment firmly at her feet. She was a selfish, grasping good-for-nothing, he decided, and it was a long time before he softened towards her again. He penned a bitter poem entitled *A Pastoral Dialogue between Richmond Lodge and Marble Hill*, in which he imagined the royal residence and that of the monarch's mistress lamenting their inevitable fall from favour now the old king was dead and his son had succeeded to the throne. The ever-acerbic Swift took the opportunity to savage his former friend and her singular lack of success in offering him a lucrative court situation.

> "Quoth Marble Hill, right well I ween,
> Your mistress now is grown a queen:
> You'll find it soon by woeful proof;
> She'll come no more beneath your roof.
>
> [...]
>
> My house was built but for a show,
> My lady's empty pockets know;
> And now she will not have a shilling,
> To raise the stairs, or build the ceiling;

For all the courtly madams round
Now pay four shillings in the pound;
'Tis come to what I always thought:
My dame is hardly worth a groat.
Had you and I been courtiers born,
We should not thus have lain forlorn:
For those we dextrous courtiers call,
Can rise upon their masters' fall.
But we, unlucky and unwise,
Must fall because our masters rise."

In fact, things were far from glamorous for Henrietta Howard, who Swift's poem mocked as a gold-digging glory seeker. She was moved into the gloomy apartments that Melusine had previously inhabited at St James Palace but found her new surroundings so damp that a constant crop of mushrooms grew between the floorboards. It was hardly the glittering life one might expect for a king's supposed favourite.

As the mushrooms flourished, so too did Queen Caroline's power over her husband's mistress. As Princess of Wales she had always relished her dominance and now, as queen, it was greater than ever. With Walpole ever at her side, the lady and the politician effectively had the country sewn up, and Henrietta's circle of political opponents and office-seekers presented a threat to the queen's power. She watched the comings and goings with growing suspicion, torn now between her desire to keep a familiar and unthreatening mistress close and by her need to ensure that nothing could undermine her own influence over her husband. Yet Caroline still held the card that might keep Henrietta in check: it was she who kept Charles Howard from seizing his wife.

As 1727 drew to a close, Henrietta finally received advice from her lawyers that Charles Howard's warrant from the Lord Chief Justice held no sway. Unless Henrietta herself consented to be taken into his custody, he could not seize her by force. Charles didn't agree and he stormed into the palace grounds and demanded that Henrietta be surrendered to him. Instead, he was chucked out on his ear.

On another occasion, Charles sought an audience with Caroline at which he warned her that he would drag Henrietta away using any means necessary. The bullying Charles, however, had reckoned without the doughty new queen. Caroline might have her faults, but she would never allow herself to be pushed around. Caroline later related the whole affair to Baron Hervey, who was no friend of Henrietta's, but certainly no friend of Charles' either.

> "Mr. Howard came to her Majesty, and said he would take his wife out of her Majesty's coach if he met her in it, she had bid him "do it if he dare;" "though," said she, "I was horribly afraid of him (for we were *tête-à-tête*) all the while I was thus playing the bully. What added to my fear upon this occasion," said the Queen, "was that, I knew him to be *so brutal*, as well as a little mad, and seldom quite sober, so I did not think it impossible but that he might throw me out of [the] window. [...] Then I told him that my resolution was positively neither to force his wife to go to him if she had no mind to it, nor to keep her if she had. He then said he would complain to the King; upon which [I] said the King had nothing to do with my servants, and for that reason he might save himself that trouble, as I was sure the King would give him no answer but that it was none of his business to concern himself with my family."[143]

Caroline had seen Charles off for now, but things had reached a head. Though Henrietta resisted the advice of her legal representatives to seek a divorce on the grounds of cruelty and abandonment, it was painfully apparent that something needed to be done to keep her husband legally at bay. Fortunately for Henrietta, the death of George I had robbed Charles of his security and of the support of the monarch who had been so happy to stir the pot of marital discord. Unsurprisingly, George II elected not to reappoint his father's troublesome retainer. For the first time, there was a real chink in Charles' armour.

Charles was still bound by the settlement reached over Audley End to pay £1,200 per year to his brother but that sum, unsurprisingly, remained routinely unpaid. James Welwood now took Henrietta's plight on and began to draw up an agreement of separation, but his unexpected death

---

143. Hervey, John and Croker, John Wilson (ed.) (1848). *Memoirs of the Reign of George the Second: From his Accession to the Death of Queen Caroline: Vol II*. London: John Murray, pp.13–15.

seemed for a time to have thwarted Henrietta's hopes. Happily for her, Thomas Trevor, 1st Baron Trevor, stepped into the breach. Lord Trevor was a distinguished legal mind who had fallen from favour under George I, but had been made Lord Privy Seal by George II. Together, Henrietta and Lord Trevor concocted a plan whereby he would ask Caroline to pay Charles £1,200 per year to retain the services of his wife. It was an odd proposition and one that failed miserably. In fact, all it managed to do was inflame the queen's annoyance towards Henrietta even further.

"That old fool My Lord Trevor came to me from *Mrs. Howard*," the queen told Hervey, "And proposed for me to give 1200/. a-year to Mr. Howard to let his wife stay with me; but as I thought I had done full enough, and that it was a little too much not only to keep the King's *guenipes*" (in English *trulls*) "under my roof, but to pay them too, I pleaded poverty to my good Lord Trevor, and said I would do anything to keep so good a servant as Mrs. Howard about me, but that for the 1200/. a-year, I really could not afford it."[144]

With no other avenue open to them, Lord Trevor and Henrietta approached the king. He grudgingly agreed to increase Henrietta's allowance by £1,200, which she would then pay directly to her husband. This agreement didn't bother Caroline as long as she didn't have to fund it herself and it would continue for as long as Charles' brother lived. When accepting the agreement, both parties confirmed that in paying the sum, Henrietta had effectively bought herself an official separation. The subsequent arrangement ensured that neither spouse could pursue the other for any monies beyond the £1,200 and that Henrietta would be free to live how and where she so desired, without any fear that her husband might try to detain her. Charles readily consented. For the first time in more than two decades, Henrietta Howard could feel *almost* free again.

---

144. Ibid., p.15.

The Countess of Suffolk

More than twenty years after the orphaned Henrietta Hobart had made her vows to the duplicitous, debauched Charles Howard, she was finally safe from his clutches. He had abused, enslaved, and ruined her, but she had emerged from the miserable marriage with something approaching a victory. Henrietta's son, Henry, was by now a young man in his twenties who had enjoyed an education at Cambridge University and had become Member of Parliament for the Devonshire constituency of Bere Alston. He was as good as a stranger. Just as his father had sworn when they parted, Henry had been raised to loathe his mother. Henrietta's hopes that her son might take it upon himself to seek her out had proven to be false. Instead, she would always be the woman who abandoned him for the promise of royal favour. The loss of her son's love was an agony to Henrietta, but she was able to content herself with lavishing all her motherly affection on little John and Dorothy Hobart, the children of her brother, John. Dorothy was to become Henrietta's pride and joy and she loved visiting her aunt at court. In her carefree, childish presence, Henrietta could forget her grumpy master and his wife.

By now Henrietta was a bona fide Georgian celebrity, whose most mundane activities were reported on widely in the press. Though she didn't court publicity, she had certainly acquired a degree of notoriety. Even the matter of her falling from her horse was worthy not only of newsprint, but also of an official apology from the man who had supposedly caused her to fall.

> "A Butcher of the Town of Windsor, who some Days ago rode hastily by Mrs. Howard first Woman of the Bedchamber to the Queen, in the Town of Kensington, and threw her from her Horse, hath, upon his asking Pardon of the Lady in a most submissive Manner, been forgiven."[145]

---

145. *London Evening Post.* 29 May 1729–31 May 1729; issue 231.

Knowing what we do of Henrietta's rather placid nature and her desire for little beyond a quiet, comfortable life, her forgiving the Windsor butcher hardly comes as a surprise.

Henrietta's deafness was by now more severe than ever and the pains in her head were so bad that she eventually submitted to surgery. She summoned physician William Cheselden and he decided that the only thing for it was to bore into Henrietta's jaw to operate on her eardrum. It was a scheme that Cheselden had championed for years, using human guinea pigs gathered from prison cells. Even in the eighteenth century, this got people talking.

"VARIOUS have been the reports and opinions of the town, concerning the operation to be performed by WILLIAM CHESELDEN, Esq; Surgeon to her Majesty, Fellow of the Royal Society, Surgeon and Lithotomist of St Thomas's Hospital, on the ears of one [Charles] Rey, a Malefactor, condemned last Sessions to be executed at Tyburn, but graciously reprieved on account of this intended Experiment. Some are of the opinion, that this ingenious Gentleman concludes, that if perforating the Drum of the ear should be found to make a man deaf, who at present enjoys the sense of hearing, the same operation will bring a person to hear, who is deaf at present. Mr. WOOLSTON is singular in his sentiment. This learned and ingenious Gentleman takes the whole story to be allegorical, and supposes, that by an operation on the Drum, is meant no more than making a great noise, But I differ from him intirely [sic]: as I know Mr. CHESELDEN to be already too famous, to stand in need of beating a drum, or sounding a trumpet to proclaim his skill in Chirurgical Operations. Besides, a drum would be a very improper Allegory for so ingenious a Gentleman to make use of: it being not only noisy, but empty."[146]

Though there were certainly those who believed that Cheselden was merely using Henrietta's suffering to further his own fame, she was sufficiently convinced by the doctor's reputation to submit to his knife. It's hard to imagine exactly what sort of agony Henrietta must have endured during the operation and ultimately it was an unsuccessful endeavour.

---

146. *Grub Street Journal*. 7 January 1731; issue 53.

"The pain of the operation was almost insupportable," she told her friend, Lady Hervey, "and the consequence was many weeks' misery, and I am not yet free from pain"[147]. When the operation failed, the only thing surgeons could suggest was that Henrietta have her apparently useless ears amputated altogether. This time she declined their services. Her recovery from the failed operation was drawn out and agonising, and for a time she grew so ill that her condition even got a brief mention in the press.

"Mrs. Howard, one of the Maids of Honour to her Majesty, is dangerously ill."[148]

Thankfully Henrietta recovered, though the pain would continue for a long time as her deafness grew ever more severe. The world was changing, and Henrietta was growing older. She was now part of the furniture at court and nobody could miss the king's declining interest in her. Instead of nightly meetings with his middle-aged mistress, George Augustus much preferred to consort with the new generation of young and outgoing maids of honour. Their relationship, never particularly passionate and certainly never particularly loving, was now one of mutual toleration and bickering. It had become in some ways rather like a dull and loveless marriage, but as long as the queen wanted it to continue, then continue it must. Until fate intervened.

"On Tuesday Night died the Right Hon. Edward Howard, Earl of Suffolk and Bindon, and Baron Howard of Walden in the County of Essex; he is succeeded in Honour and Estate by his Brother, Charles Howard, now Earl of Suffolk and Bindon, who was a Groom of the Bed-Chamber to the late King, and whose Countess was one of the Bed-Chamber Women to her present Majesty till yesterday, when her Ladyship resign'd that Place."[149]

Edward Howard, 8th Earl of Suffolk, died on 22 June 1731, and his brother, the dissolute Charles, succeeded to the title as 9th Earl. Though

---

147. Henrietta Howard to Lady Hervey, 1728, BL, Add. MS 22626, fol. 94.
148. *Daily Post.* 1 August 1728.
149. *London Evening Post.* 22 June 1731–24 June 1731; issue 557.

the couple were by now separated, Henrietta still acquired the title of Countess of Suffolk at her husband's succession. The legal battle between the two brothers over Audley End had driven a vast wedge between them and the late earl took his final revenge from beyond the grave. Having no heirs of her own, he left what money he still possessed after the legal bills had been settled to his sister-in-law, Henrietta Howard, the new Countess of Suffolk. The 8th Earl wisely made Henrietta's friends the Duke of Argyll and Lord Ilay, his trustees, certain that they would see off any challenge from Charles when he made his inevitable attempt to seize her £3,000 inheritance.

The title of Countess of Suffolk brought with it benefits that Henrietta knew would make her life far more comfortable. Chief among them was a change in the role she occupied in the royal household, for no countess could possibly be expected to toil on her knees as a Woman of the Bedchamber. Now Caroline had two choices. First, and Henrietta's preferred option, was that she be relived of her duties and allowed to enter into a private life with the blessing of the queen. The second, which Caroline favoured, was to retain Henrietta's services, but promote her to a more senior position. No doubt Henrietta prayed for the former, but Caroline chose the latter. She offered Henrietta a choice between the roles of Lady of the Bedchamber or Mistress of the Robes. The latter was the most senior role in the queen's gift and a position that was currently held by the less experienced Duchess of Dorset. Henrietta accepted the more prestigious, easier role, and wrote to John Gay to share not only her triumphs, but her worries too.

"I shall let you know that I have kissed hands for the place of Mistress of the Robes. Her Majesty did me the honour to give me the choice of Lady of the Bedchamber, or that, which I find so much more agreeable to me, that I did not take one moment to consider of it. The Duchess of Dorset resigned it for me; and every thing [sic] as yet promises more happiness for the latter part of my life than I have yet had a prospect of. Seven nights' quiet sleep, and seven easy days have almost worked a miracle upon me; for if I cannot say I am perfectly well, yet it is certain even my pain is more supportable than it was. I shall now often visit Marble Hill; my time is become very much my own, and I shall see it without the dread of being obliged to sell it to answer the engagement I had put myself under to avoid a greater evil. Mr. H[oward] took possession of body and goods, and was not prevailed upon till yesterday to resign the former for burial. Poor Lord Suffolk took so much care in the will he made, that the best lawyers say it must stand good. I am persuaded it will be tried to the uttermost."[150]

Henrietta's new role was a world away from that which she had occupied before. Now the queen's hygiene and tooth picking were no longer any of her concern. Instead her job was to care for Caroline's wardrobe and lay out her clothes and jewels for the day, which was hardly an arduous task. Now her husband was the earl, there was no longer any requirement for Henrietta to pay him the £1,200 that had been agreed to when they separated either, so that money could now go straight into her own coffers. The one thing that Henrietta couldn't get used to was the fact that her friends now began to address her formally as a countess. Eventually she chided John Gay with a good-natured threat that, "If you do not leave off ladyship, [I] shall make you go supperless to bed."[151]

When Henrietta had written to Gay and speculated that her husband would do all he could to challenge his late brother's will, she had proven that even after more than a decade of separation, she still knew her spouse well. Charles did indeed pursue Henrietta for the money her brother-in-law had left to her. In fact, he would do so fruitlessly for the scant years that remained of his life. Henrietta had been expecting nothing less and was happy to leave the legal tangles up to her representatives whilst she settled into a slower pace of life as the Mistress of the Robes. Now she was no longer required to be in constant attendance on the queen, she could spend more time than ever before at Marble Hill, making it into the nest she had always longed for.

The house later became the home of Maria Fitzherbert, secret wife of George IV, and it is a place that has caught the imaginations of many. More than a century after Henrietta's death, Marble Hill came onto the property market and one commentator summed up the mystique and

---

150. Henrietta Howard to John Gay, 29 June 1731, BL, Add. MS 22626, fol. 53.
151. Melville, Lewis (1921). *Life and Letters of John Gay*. London: Daniel O'Connor, p.131.

glamour that had attached itself to Henrietta's beloved home over the years.

> "It was designed by Lord Burlington and Lord Pembroke for Henrietta Howard, who became Countess of Suffolk. This was in the reign of George the Second, who contributed twelve thousand pounds towards the building. Mahogany was used for the floors of the principal rooms and in the grand staircase. According to Cobbett, it was Pope who superintended the layout out of the gardens, while Dean Swift stocked the cellars. The former remain to testify to the taste of the great poet, but the contents of the huge cellars have long ago disappeared, and we in this later day have only the gout to remind us of the great drinking capacity of our forefathers. I have passed the grand old house many a time when on the river. It stands nearly hidden by great trees, but there is a terrace coming down to the water's edge, where doubtless in the old days of the house's prosperity many a gaily bewigged gallant handed the ladies, ravishing in hoops, furbelows, powdered hair and patches, into his boat and bade the waterman row to Kew or Richmond."[152]

Intrigue and romance aside, all Henrietta really wanted was the freedom to make her own way. Over the years her true friends at court had dwindled in number as they married and left the queen's service, but Marble Hill offered a second chance. Now she was spending more time at Twickenham, her social circle there began to grow accordingly and chief among her friends was Lady Elizabeth Germain. Known to all as Betty, Lady Elizabeth had been maid of honour to Queen Anne so knew all about serving a sometimes-capricious mistress. She and Henrietta were soon fast friends, but little suspected that they would one day be closer still. Henrietta, the widowed mistress of a king who could by now barely tolerate her presence, might be expected to have given up on romance. Romance, however, had not given up on her.

Betty's brother was George Berkeley, a politician who had once been loyal to Robert Walpole but had since allied himself with Walpole's opponents, incurring the wrath of the powerful politician and his cronies.

---

152. *Wrexham Weekly Advertiser*. 2 June 1888; volume 40.

Since 1723 he had been Master Keeper and Governor of St Katharine's Hospital in London. He was a little younger than Henrietta and as good company as her late husband had been bad. She soon counted him among her close friends and when their mutual confidant John Gay died in 1732, a heartbroken Henrietta personally asked George Berkeley to serve as one of Gay's pall bearers. It was proof of the high regard in which she held him.

George and Henrietta's friendship was strictly platonic at the outset, but there is evidence that they became close quickly. George interested himself in Henrietta's welfare in a way that neither her husband nor the king ever had. When he wrote to a friend regarding Henrietta's decision to take the trip to Bath that precluded her eventual retirement from court, it was clear that he had her welfare on his mind.

> "I believe the secret of this journey is, that she has a mind to get out of her lodgings at Kensington, which being at least three feet underground, are at this time of the year vary damp and unwholesome, especially to her ill health, not in a very strong constitution; besides showing she will not be such a slave to the court as she has been, having never been six weeks in the whole absent from it in twenty year's service."[153]

George's concern for Henrietta's wellbeing was an indication of her how close they had quietly become. It was also her first step towards a new life.

---

153. George Berkeley to anonymous, August 1734, BL, Add. MS 22628, fol. 100.

The Merry Widow

"Last Friday died at Bath the Earl of Suffolk."[154]

And just like that, with one throwaway line in a newspaper, the world learned of the end of the man who had tormented Henrietta Howard for decades. Charles Howard died as he had lived, heavily in debt, and those debts now passed on to his son, Henry, 10th Earl of Suffolk. Audley End needed a sound financial brain to manage it and Charles, who was singularly talented at throwing away cash, had not been the man to do that. Young Henry, on the other hand, had inherited his mother's good head for finances. The 10th Earl of Suffolk would prove to be the custodian that Audley End needed and he managed to coax the great house back into profitability, perhaps thanks to the hard-headed approach that he also employed with his mother, who he refused to acknowledge. She wasn't even present when he married Sarah Inwen, a wealthy brewer's daughter, on 13 May 1735. In some ways Henry certainly took after his late father, because Sarah's family fortune made her a very attractive proposition indeed.

Henrietta knew better than to expect any reconciliation with her son, but there was another source of delight in her life now. George Berkeley had become a closer friend than ever, a man she exchanged playful letters with, and to whom she was not indebted in any way. He was tender and teasing, enquiring after jokey court gossip before seeking Henrietta's assurance that she was in good health and spirits. When George asked after her head and face, perhaps a reference not only to her ongoing headaches but also to Cheselden's brutal operation, Henrietta told him, "I think the less that is said of either is the better; they are neither pleasant nor profitable to others nor the owner."[155] We might imagine, however,

---

154. *St James's Evening Post*. 29 September 1733–2 October 1733; issue 2859.
155. Henrietta Howard to George Berkeley, 22 June 1734, BL, Add. MS 22629, fol. 34.

that George Berkeley was minded to disagree with that particular sentiment. Though at odds with Walpole's powerful faction he sought neither advancement nor influence through his friendship with the king's mistress, but instead delighted in her company for its own sake. His attentions, combined with frequent visits from her niece, Dorothy, only increased Henrietta's longing for retirement. It wasn't long before her friends noticed the burgeoning friendship too.

> "I have made your compliments to my friend; but I am not sure that she approves this regular correspondence; as she was always a much better, so she was always a much stricter woman than I am."[156]

Henrietta signed off the letter with a flirtatious admonishment that, "I was surprised at your ill-breeding, to send a letter without an envelope."[157] One might almost imagine she was enjoying playing the coquette after decades in the sensible Swiss cantons.

Whether Queen Caroline liked it or not, Henrietta decided to spend the late summer and early autumn of 1734 in Bath, where she revelled in the company of her oldest friends. The healing properties of the spa town were just what she needed to help with the recurrent headaches which had begun to blight her again. In Bath she could relax and indulge herself in society circles, even though she continued to maintain that all-important air of neutral good humour that had served her so well. She also cooked up a plan to capitalise on the presence of many of the king's natural political enemies as well as his gossipy daughter, Princess Amelia.

Henrietta courted the company of George Augustus' most loathed opponents, including Lord Bolingbroke, who had benefitted from Melusine's favour years earlier. She made sure that Princess Amelia heard of her eyebrow-raising social circle too, certain that she wouldn't be able to resist sharing the gossip with the king. It was all groundwork for her eventual retirement. Everyone knew that George Augustus was tired of his mistress, it wouldn't take much to convince him to give her the heave-ho. George Augustus' nightly meetings with Henrietta had dwindled away to almost nothing whilst Lady Bristol, whose room was next door

---

156. Henrietta Howard to George Berkeley, 25 June 1734, BL, Add. MS 22629, fol. 36.
157. Ibid.

to Henrietta's, reported that she often heard the couple engaged in tense exchanges that ended with the king telling his mistress, "That is none of your business, madam; you have nothing to do with that."

The trip to Bath felt like a natural turning point for their relationship. It was certainly an overture to the final curtain and with valuable time to think, Henrietta resolved upon securing the one thing she had wanted for years: retirement.

When Henrietta returned to the court, she was surprised to find that the king had grown cooler than ever towards her. His disinterest seemed far too pointed to be a simple response to Princess Amelia's gossip and Henrietta began to fear that the ruse she had worked in Bath, when she mingled with George Augustus' opponents to further encourage him to end their relationship, had backfired. After her return from her trip to the spa town, the king barely spoke to or acknowledged Henrietta at all, which left her in a panic. Though she desperately wanted to leave the queen's service and the king's bed, she had to do so on good terms. That meant finding out exactly what had happened during her absence. Henrietta had no choice but to ask George Augustus what was troubling him, but she was careful to be appropriately submissive when she wrote to enquire what she had done to deserve his coolness.

"I ask, Sir, but what your meanest, your guiltiest, subject can claim. A malefactor cannot suffer till his accusers prove their charge. No power, no greatness can screen in this case the informers; they must give evidence or the accused is acquitted; the guilt of falsehood falls (as it truly ought) on the heads of the accusers. Is it, then, too much for me to ask, and after the attachment I have had for your Majesty for twenty years? or [sic] can I expect less from your justice, your honour, or your former goodness shown to me than to know for what I now suffer the loss of your favour and the honour I had of having some share in your friendship?"[158]

Henrietta then went to the queen and, over a long and difficult conversation, asked Caroline what might possibly have happened to change the atmosphere so much at the palace. She also sought the queen's permission to retire from her duties. Caroline, however, either could not

---

158. Henrietta Howard to George II, November 1734, BL, Add. MS 22627, fol. 6.

or would not offer her any insight. Instead, she told Henrietta that it was nothing but her imagination playing tricks. "I am your friend, your best friend," the queen assured her, no doubt with all the sincerity of a spider soothing its lunch. "Oh my dear Lady Suffolk, you do not know how differently, when you are out [retired from court], people will behave."

Henrietta was desperate and though Caroline was unmoving, so too was her servant. Eventually the queen secured Henrietta's promise that she would take a week to consider if retirement was what she really wanted. No doubt Caroline intended to spend that same week convincing George Augustus that he should show Henrietta some warmth to keep her in the royal bosom. All she had achieved really was to delay the inevitable.

When the queen went to her husband and told him that Henrietta had tried to retire but that she had been able to temporarily prevent it, his response was far from grateful. Instead of thanking Caroline for keeping his long-serving mistress close by, George Augustus bellowed, "What the devil did you mean by trying to make an old, dull, deaf, peevish beast stay and plague me when I had so good an opportunity of getting rid of her?"[159]. It was the last thing Caroline had expected to hear and it was proof, if she really needed it, that the status quo could no longer be preserved. Henrietta Howard was released from the royal household with her reputation intact, though she never discovered the cause of the king's sudden coolness. When she departed in November 1734, Henrietta left a letter for George Augustus that showed she had retained her good grace against all the odds.

> "To have constantly done my duty in those places her Majesty has honoured me with, and to prove to you with duty the most sincere, the most tender friendship (pardon this expression) attended with the highest sense of gratitude for the honour of your esteem has been my business for twenty years past [...] The years to come must be employed in the painful wish to forget you and my friend; but no fears can ever make me forget you as my king, as no usage can prevent my warmest wishes for your happiness or put an end to that profound duty, respect and submission."[160]

---

159. Croker, John Wilson (ed.) (1848). *Memoirs of the Reign of George II from his Accession to the Death of Queen Caroline by John, Lord Hervey: Vol II*. London: John Murray, p.179.

160. Henrietta Howard to George II, November 1734, BL, Add. MS 22627, fol. 6.

With that, to the great surprise of the chattering classes, Lady Suffolk left the royal court. "Her going from Court was the silliest thing she could do,"[161] Queen Caroline told Lord Hervey, but one suspects that Henrietta would happily have begged to differ. Armed with the key to Marble Hill and a £2,000 pension paid by the king, she packed her bags for good.

"I have been a slave twenty years without ever receiving a reason for any one thing I ever was obliged to do," Henrietta wrote, "I have now a mind to take the pleasure, once in my life, of absolute power"[162]. Free at last of her husband, her patron, and her queen, she wanted to taste everything that the world had to offer.

As for George Augustus, his bed wasn't empty for long. During a trip to Hanover he entered into an intrigue with Amalie von Wallmoden, the niece of Melusine von der Schulenberg. She was two decades his junior and by 1736 had become the mother of a son by King George II. Amalie was everything Caroline feared, and she would continue as George Augustus' mistress until his death more than twenty years later. Created Countess of Yarmouth in recognition of her loyal service to the crown, Amalie proved to have far more staying power than Henrietta Howard ever did. If anyone had cause to mourn Henrietta's departure, it was Queen Caroline.

161. Croker, John Wilson (ed.) (1848). *Memoirs of the Reign of George II from his Accession to the Death of Queen Caroline by John, Lord Hervey: Vol II*. London: John Murray, p.12.
162. Howard, Henrietta, Countess of Suffolk (1824). *Letters to and from Henrietta, Countess of Suffolk, Vol I*. London: John Murray, p.262.

Mrs Berkeley

"My old mistress has married that old rake George Berkeley, and I am very glad of it. I would not make such a gift to my friends, and when my enemies rob me, please God it will always be in this same manner."

Though George II was never less of a gentleman than when he reported Henrietta's marriage to his wife, Queen Caroline, we might detect a certain hint of sour grapes. It would have come as no surprise to the Countess of Suffolk, retired bastion of the royal household, that her departure from the queen's service and the king's company set tongues wagging. Her friends were sorry for the change in her circumstances, sympathising that she had been so ill-used after such a long and loyal period of service, but when Lady Betty Germain wrote to Swift, it was clear that Henrietta had no regrets at all. The former royal mistress was mistress of herself at last.

"I truly think she was heartily sorry to be obliged, by ill-usage, to quit a master and mistress that she had served so justly and loved so well. However, she now has much more ease and liberty, and accordingly her health is better."[163]

One might have expected Henrietta to hasten to Marble Hill as soon as her bags were packed, but instead she went to St James's Square and the home of her brother John. Here she could decompress after years under the royal yoke, safe in the company of her last living sibling and especially her beloved niece, Dorothy. After several weeks in her happy new situation Henrietta finally settled into her sanctuary at Marble Hill, where the Thames flowed past the very end of the elegant gardens. She

---

163. Wilkes, Thomas (ed.) (1767). *The Works of the Reverend Dr Jonathan Swift: Vol XVI.* Dublin: George Faulkner, p.89.

didn't settle there alone though. On 26 June 1735, she married George Berkeley.

"The Hon. George Berkeley, Esq; younger Brother of the Earl of Berkeley, and Member of Parliament for Heydon in Yorkshire, was [...] marry'd to the Right Hon. The Countess Dowager of Suffolk."[164]

"Mr. Berkeley was neither young, handsome, healthy, nor rich," wrote the acerbic pen of Lord Hervey, "Which made people wonder what induced Lady Suffolk's prudence to deviate into this unaccountable piece of folly: some imagined it was to persuade the world that nothing criminal had ever passed between her and the King; others that it was to pique the King: if this was her reason, she succeeded very ill in her design"[165].

Her friend and new sister-in-law, Betty, fancied in her tongue-in-cheek fashion that she knew better what lay behind the surprising decision to marry. Her brother might be a middle-aged bachelor, but that didn't mean that he couldn't still fall head over heels for his bride.

"The town is surprized [sic], and the town talks, as the town loves to do, upon these ordinary extraordinary occasions. She is indeed four or five years older than he, and no more; but for all that, he hath appeared to all the world, as well as me, to have long had (that is ever since she hath been a widow, so pray don't mistake me) a most violent passion for her, as well as esteem and value for her numberless good qualities. These things well considered I do not think they have above ten to one against their being very happy, and if they should not be so, I shall heartily wish him hanged, because I am sure it will be wholly his fault."[166]

Despite Hervey's inevitable reservations, Henrietta and George's friends were delighted for the newlyweds. It was not so strange to them to imagine

164. *London Evening Post.* 12 July 1735–15 July 1735; issue 1194.
165. Croker, John Wilson (ed.) (1848). *Memoirs of the Reign of George II from his Accession to the Death of Queen Caroline by John, Lord Hervey: Vol II.* London: John Murray, pp.10–11.
166. Wilkes, Thomas (ed.) (1767). *The Works of the Reverend Dr Jonathan Swift: Vol XVI.* Dublin: George Faulkner, pp.111–112.

that Henrietta, who was by then 45 and had never really known love, was so keen to embrace it when it came along. The Berkeleys hosted friends at Marble Hill and in their London residence in Savile Street – now Savile Row – which Henrietta had purchased for £3,000 soon after she left court. They even travelled to France, where they spent the summer of 1736 visiting friends. For the first time, Henrietta could really enjoy the life she had so longed for. It's little wonder that Pope commented affectionately that, "There is a greater Court now at Marble Hill than at Kensington."[167]

Henrietta's joy was complete when her niece and nephew, Dorothy, then 15, and John, 13, came to Marble Hill to live with her and George. Their own mother had died in 1727 and although John had remarried the following year, he was happy for his children to live with his sister. Perhaps he also suspected that they might provide her with some means to fill the void that the loss of her only son Henry had created.

Henrietta was still enjoying a blissful married life in 1737 when Queen Caroline, her old employer and tormentor, died after a protracted and agonising operation on an old hernia. The king was heartbroken at the loss of his greatest confidante and the woman who many believed had been the true power behind the throne. At home in Twickenham, Henrietta could absorb the news in her own time. She had no official role to play, after all.

The only real cloud hanging over Marble Hill was Henrietta and George's worsening health problems. George had lived with gout for years but now it was worse than ever, exacerbated by all the celebratory dinners and gatherings that he and his happy wife attended. Henrietta, meanwhile, had never really been free from her headaches, and by 1741, she was suffering from an attack of rheumatism so severe that she couldn't even hold her pen. When her doctor suggested laudanum Henrietta initially resisted, but how long she could continue to struggle on for was debateable. Whenever George Berkeley had to leave Henrietta to visit his Yorkshire constituency in Hedon, Betty became her closest confidante. In her letters to George she informed him of Henrietta's struggles with ill health and told him her doctor had drawn a blister behind her ear, which

---

167. Warner, Rebecca (ed.) (1817). *Original Letters.* London: Longman, Hurst, Rees, Orme, and Brown, p.52.

seemed to be doing no harm and perhaps a little good. If nothing else Henrietta was finally able to sleep, which she had not been able to do for days on end.

Henrietta and George kept up a constant and lively correspondence when they couldn't be together. Even when suffering, she retained a gentle humour when discussing her woes with her adored husband.

> "My head is pretty easy, but my charming face, which, to be sure, gives pain to others, now fully revenges their quarrel. But I have yet resisted laudanum: how long my resolution will hold, God knows, for the temptation is at this moment very strong."[168]

When Henrietta's health grew troublesome again, she dictated her letters to his sister, Betty. In them she discussed "our little family" with tender affection, as proud of her niece and nephew as any parent would be, whilst George replied with news of his journey to Yorkshire. What really emerges from their correspondence is how much the couple missed one another and longed to be together again. Henrietta implored George to hurry home, lest "you will be visited by a more dreadful officer than any the law produces – an incensed wife"[169]. It was like a permanent honeymoon period, but there was heartbreak on the road ahead.

---

168. Henrietta Howard to George Berkeley, 18 April 1741, BL, Add. MS 22629, fol. 52.
169. Ibid.

Twilight

"Last Monday died, and not before, at his Seat near Saffron Walden in Essex, the Right Hon. The Earl of Suffolk. His Lordship married a Daughter of Thomas Inwin, Esq; late of the Borough of Southwark, by whom he has no issue."[170]

When Henry Howard died, he had been a stranger to his mother for years. Though his marriage had been financially astute it had not resulted in any children, so at his death the title passed to the great-grandson of the very 1st Earl of Suffolk. Henry was just 39 when he died in the Spring of 1745 and with his death, the last shred of hope that there might be a reconciliation also went to the grave. Yet it had been decades since mother and son had seen one another and perhaps, in some strange way, Henrietta had already grieved for his loss. Though the blow was still hard, the fact that she had a loving husband and a sanctuary to call her own was no doubt a great tonic to Henrietta. The same could not be said for the second tragedy to hit her in the space of eighteen short months.

"On Wednesday last died at Bath the Hon. George Berkeley, Esq; Member of Parliament for Heydon in Yorkshire, Master of St. Katherine's near the Tower, and Brother to the late Earl of Berkeley. He married the Dowager Countess of Suffolk, but has left no issue."[171]

George Berkeley, Henrietta's best friend and loving husband of 11 years, died on 29 October 1746. He left everything he possessed to his adored, distraught wife. In George, Henrietta had found the companionship and love that she had never known before. She would not marry again.

---

170. *Daily Gazetteer.* 24 April 1745; issue 5017.
171. *General London Evening Mercury.* 1 November 1746; issue 549.

As Henrietta approached her sixtieth year, she retired to her beloved home of Marble Hill. The glittering social life she and George had enjoyed together held less appeal without him, but Henrietta was not the sort of woman who would ever become a recluse. Instead she continued to host her friends and to visit them too. Home was hardly quiet anyway, especially with Dorothy for company. The young lady's father, John, was created Earl of Buckinghamshire in 1746 and with his promotion, Dorothy became a tempting prospect for fortune hunting suitors. It was Henrietta who steered her through the choppy waters of romance, but one man who came calling at Marble Hill was more interested in Henrietta than her adopted daughter.

Horace Walpole, Robert's son, moved to the picturesque estate of Strawberry Hill at the age of 30 and set about transforming it into a fairy tale landscape of Gothic delights. Walpole was an eminently sociable fellow and he soon called on the Dowager Countess of Suffolk, intrigued by the woman who had never been a favourite of his father. Walpole's writings provide us with a wealth of marvellous court gossip and he revelled in the company of courtly ladies, rejoicing in their stories of the kings and consorts they'd known. In Henrietta and Betty he found his perfect friends and soon he was virtually part of the family. The trio took tea together as Henrietta listened to Walpole's questions through her ear trumpet and regaled him with stories of her life in the royal household.

Once Dorothy married and set out on her own life, Henrietta became the grande dame of Marble Hill. She was constantly welcoming visitors, from old friends to her ever-loyal neighbour and chronicler, Horace Walpole. When her health began to decline she came to rely on Walpole to take down her dictated letters and he fretted endlessly whenever she suffered any ailment, which happened with all too increasing regularity as the years passed.

With the death of her brother John in 1756, Henrietta alone remained of the eight children who had begun their journey so many years earlier at Blickling Hall. In the decades that had passed from those bleak early days, their lives had changed immeasurably. Though her nephew was one of the new generation of courtiers who now bowed to the elderly George II, Henrietta never felt the urge to return to her old haunts at Kensington Palace and St James's. She did, however, see her former patron one final time before they parted forever.

During a trip to London in late 1760, Henrietta visited Kensington to view the gardens. Unbeknownst to her, the king was also making a visit and by the time she discovered his approach, it was too late to flee. Caught in the melee of coaches, Henrietta prepared herself to face George Augustus and his companion, Amalie, Countess of Yarmouth, for the first time in more than a quarter of a century. She related the rueful story to Horace Walpole.

> "Two days before [King George II] died, [Henrietta] went to make a visit at Kensington, not knowing of the review; she found herself hemmed in by coaches, and was close to him, whom she had not seen for so many years, and to my lady Yarmouth; but they did not know her; it struck her."[172]

How painful it must have been for Henrietta not to have been recognised by the very man who used to pace the floor in agitation as he waited to be admitted to her chambers. It saved them both an awkward encounter but there must have been a sting of humiliation in being passed by. Henrietta had become invisible. Just two days later the old king died, collapsing on the floor of his toilet as his valet waited outside. George Augustus, once the glittering centre of a fashionable young court, had followed his father into grumpy old age. Bad-tempered, miserly, and given to tantrums to the end, he was 76 when he died.

Though George Augustus and Henrietta had long since ceased to be even acquaintances, she had continued to receive a pension from the royal household ever since her departure. With George II's death, that ceased. Though Henrietta's funding was cut off, the new king was keen not only to acknowledge her existence but to draw on her knowledge as a former and exemplary Mistress of the Robes. Not long after he succeeded to the throne, King George III called upon Henrietta to advise his new wife, Queen Charlotte, on her role at the forthcoming coronation. Henrietta memorialised the occasion in answer to an official request from the palace.

> "At the late queen's coronation the Duchess of Dorset was mistress of the robes; but Mrs. Howard, bedchamber-woman, having had

---

172. Walpole, Horace (1837). *Correspondence of Horace Walpole with George Montagu Esq: Vol II*. London: Henry Colburn, p.46.

all things belonging to that office for many years under her care, received her majesty's commands to provide every thing proper for her majesty's dress for the coronation, and to inquire into all particulars necessary for the queen to know.

[…]

The night before the coronation the queen's order to all her servants, except the bedchamber-woman, was to be at Westminster in the places assigned them, at the hour appointed for their summons; and at a little after seven o'clock the next morning her majesty, being in an undress, but every thing new, went into her chair (not a state one) with the curtains drawn; her lord chamberlain in a hackney chair before, her majesty and Mrs. Howard in hers behind.

[…]

As soon as her majesty got to Westminster, Mrs. Howard dressed her, assisted only by those who belonged to the office. Mrs. Herbert, the other bedchamber-woman, came in, but being in her full dress, could not assist. As soon as the queen came into the room where the peeresses were assembled, from that time the Duchess of Dorset assisted as mistress of the robes."[173]

Henrietta was present at the coronation dressed in the fine robes of a countess, her hair styled by Horace Walpole, but it was a rare ceremonial outing for the lady of Marble Hill. She preferred to remain at home with her friends, hosting little gatherings and delighting in the company of her latest houseguest. Just as she had once brought Dorothy and John to Marble Hill, now she shared her house with Henrietta, the only child of Dorothy and her husband, Colonel Charles Hotham. She adored the little girl, lavishing her with affection as young Henrietta filled the house with joy; there was never any chance that Marble Hill would lose its sparkle.

---

173. Howard, Henrietta, Countess of Suffolk (1824). *Letters to and from Henrietta, Countess of Suffolk, Vol II*. London: John Murray, pp.262–264.

Henrietta was as close as ever to her nephew, John, 2nd Earl of Buckinghamshire, too. He had followed the family tradition and entered the world of politics, eventually pursuing a career in the diplomatic service. He regaled his aunt with news from Russia, where he was serving in the often thankless role of the United Kingdom's ambassador, and shared with her his thoughts on the sometimes perplexing and challenging St Petersburg court. John missed home and hearth dreadfully and admitted, "I try to make the most of what is; regret only one year [...] of all that is past; and have no very sanguine hopes of the future."[174]

Whenever Henrietta referred to her advancing years, John dismissed her worries with charm and good humour, assuring his aunt that she was as keen, healthy, and witty as ever. She and her old correspondent, Lord Chesterfield, still wrote to one another as playfully as ever too, adopting the guises of a maid in the Suffolk household and a footman in the Chesterfield residence. Elderly they might be, but it's rather cheering to realise that in their own respectable way, the courtiers of Kensington Palace had never quite grown up.

Though Henrietta had lost her hearing, her wits remained pin sharp even as her body grew more frail than ever. In 1764 Horace Walpole sent an account of Henrietta's agonising state of health to his friend, George Montagu. That she lived for a further three years seems little short of a miracle.

"[She is] past seventy six; and, what is more, much worse than I was for added to her deafness, she has been confined these three weeks with the gout in her eyes, and was actually then in misery, and had been without sleep. What spirits, and cleverness, and imagination, at that age, and under those afflicting circumstances! You reconnoitre her old court knowledge, how charmingly she has applied it! Do you wonder I pass so many hours and evenings with her? Alas I had like to have lost her this morning! They had poulticed her feet to draw the gout downwards, and began to succeed yesterday, but to-day it flew up into her head, and she was almost in convulsions with the agony, and screamed dreadfully; proof enough how ill she was for

---

174. The Earl of Buckinghamshire to Henrietta Howard, 18 November 1763, BL, Add.
     MS 22629, fol. 95.

her patience and good-breeding make her for ever sink and conceal what she feels. This evening the gout has been driven back to her foot, and I trust she is out of danger. Her loss would be irreparable to me at Twickenham, where she is by far the most rational and agreeable company I have."[175]

Henrietta's health was in terminal decline. She was confined to her bed for long periods with gout in her joints and eyes and was forced to put her Marble Hill gatherings on hold. If nothing else can be taken as evidence of how ill she had become, that is surely proof.

---

175. Walpole, Horace (1837). *Correspondence of Horace Walpole with George Montagu Esq: Vol II*. London: Henry Colburn, p.231.

The Late Countess

It seems somehow fitting that Henrietta spent one of her last evenings in the company of her beloved Horace Walpole. In the days after her death, he wrote an account of their final meeting and her poor health, but he hadn't anticipated her imminent demise. His grief for his unlikely friend ran deep.

> "Strawberry Hill, July 29 1767
> I am very sorry that I must speak of a loss that [has] deprived of a most agreeable friend, with whom I passed here many hours. I need not say I mean poor Lady Suffolk. I was with her two hours on Saturday night; and indeed found her much changed, though I did not apprehend her in danger. I was going to say she complained – but you know she never did complain – of the gout and rheumatism all over her, particularly in her face. It was a cold night, and she sat below stairs when she should have been in bed; and I doubt this want of care was prejudicial.
>
> [...]
>
> In truth, I never knew a woman more respectable for her honour and principles, and have lost few persons in my life whom I shall miss so much."[176]

Henrietta died on 26 July 1767, after spending the evening at home in the company of old friends. Perhaps fittingly, she was not alone at the time of her death but was instead with William Chetwynd, recently created 3rd Viscount Chetwynd. He had been a friend of her late husband who had remained close to Henrietta after George's death. Henrietta and

---

176. Ibid., pp.341–343.

Lord Chetwynd had been warming themselves beside the fire when she decided to take supper in her chambers. The viscount escorted Henrietta upstairs and helped her to a chair. As she sat, she clutched her side and swooned. Within half an hour, Henrietta Howard, the Dowager Countess of Suffolk, was dead.

> "On Sunday night died at her seat at Marble Hill, near Richmond, in the 86th year of her age, the lady of the Right Hon. the Earl of Suffolk. She was many years Keeper of the Wardrobe to her late Majesty Queen Caroline."[177]

In her will, Henrietta bequeathed the bulk of her respectable 60-acre estate to her niece, Dorothy, and Dorothy's daughter, Henrietta Hotham, whilst she left Marble Hill to her nephew, John. The will stipulated that her cherished estate and all the contents of the house were to remain together and that, should John die without male heirs, then the estate and its contents would pass to young Henrietta and from there, along the female line of the family. Henrietta had known to her cost that women all too often lacked resources to call their own.

Henrietta had lived through tumultuous times. She had watched the dawn of the modern era and played a personal role as the Hanoverians made themselves comfortable on the British throne, but it had taken her decades to achieve what she really dreamt of. With the key to her own front door at Marble Hill and the companionship of her beloved George Berkeley, Henrietta's dreams finally came true. She outlived her husband by 21 years but at her death they could finally be reunited. Henrietta was laid beside her adored spouse in the family vault at Berkeley Castle, where they rest together to this day.

---

177. *London Evening Post.* 28 July 1767–30 July 1767; issue 4473.

Afterword

There is something about the word *mistress*. It carries with it centuries of weight and meaning, and a whole world of unspoken sentiment. For the royal mistress those unspoken sentiments are magnified, and every move made by the woman at the side of a monarch takes on a new significance in the eyes of those who know them, who seek to profit from them, or who oppose them.

In Melusine von der Schulenberg and Henrietta Howard we see two women who circumstance and time dictated were to become the mistresses of powerful, deeply flawed men. Swept up in events that changed the face of the country and sometimes even the world, they were a quiet constant in the lives of George I and George II. One became as good as a wife, a lifelong companion who bore her partner three children and commanded the most ambitious courtiers as surely as any queen. The other was driven by different impulses, seeking safety and security as she fled a husband who had mistreated her for years. Yet in Melusine and Henrietta, there were as many similarities as there were differences. They survived by playing the game of court politics in their own way, by soothing bad-tempered royal brows and enduring criticism and suspicion not only from those who knew them, but also from those strangers who sought to condemn them as women who had dared to rise above their station.

Melusine and Henrietta were not the only mistresses of their respective kings, but they made an indelible impression on the royal households that knew them. Today the Duchess of Kendal and the Countess of Suffolk are as intriguing as ever. Their lives tell us much about the lot of the female favourite and the monarchs who they served. Few had better access to the ear of the sovereign than they did, and few career politicians could boast their diplomatic skills. They set the stage for a great many mistresses to come.

Bibliography

Agnew, David CA. *Protestant Exiles from France in the Reign of Louis XIV: Vol I.*
London: Reeves & Turner, 1871.

Ainsworth, William Harrison. *The South-Sea Bubble, Vol. I.* Leipzig: Bernhard
Tauchnitz, 1868.

Ainsworth, William Harrison. *The South-Sea Bubble, Vol. II.* Leipzig: Bernhard
Tauchnitz, 1868.

Aldridge, David Denis. *Admiral Sir John Norris and the British Naval Expeditions
to the Baltic Sea 1715–1727.* Nordic Academic Press: Lund, 2009.

Andréadès, AM. *History of the Bank of England, 1640–1903.* Abingdon: Frank
Cass & Co, Ltd, 1966.

Anonymous. *Belgravia, Vol LXXVII.* London: FW White & Co, 1892.

Anonymous. *The Georgian Era, Vol I.* London: Vizetelly, Branston and Co, 1832.

Anonymous. *Letters, in the Original, with Translations, and Messages, that Passed
Between the King, Queen, Prince, and Princess of Wales.* London: S Osborn, 1737.

Anonymous. *The Life of the Princess of Zell, Wife of George I King of England.*
London: Privately published, undated.

Anonymous (ed.). *University Library of Autobiography: Vol V.* New York, F Tyler
Daniels, 1918.

Arkell, Ruby Lillian. *Caroline of Ansbach: George the Second's Queen.* Oxford:
Oxford University Press, 1939.

Balen, Malcolm. *Very English Deceit.* London: Fourth Estate: 2009.

Ballantyne, Archibald. *Lord Carteret: A Political Biography.* London: Richard
Bentley & Son, 1887.

Beacock Fryer, Mary, Bousfield, Arthur and Toffoli, Garry. *Lives of the Princesses
of Wales.* Toronto: Dundurn Press, 1983.

Beattie, John M. *The English Court in the Reign of George I.* Cambridge:
Cambridge University Press, 1967.

Beatty, Michael A. *The English Royal Family of America, from Jamestown to the
American Revolution.* Jefferson: McFarland & Co, 2003.

Belsham, W. *Memoirs of the Kings of Great Britain of the House of Brunswic-
Luneburg, Vol I.* London: C Dilly, 1793.

Belsham, William. *Memoirs of the Kings of Great Britain of the House of Brunswic-
Luneburg, Vol II.* London: C Dilly, 1796.

Benjamin, Lewis Saul. *The First George in Hanover and England, Volume I.*
London: Charles Scribner's Sons, 1909.

Benjamin, Lewis Saul. *The First George in Hanover and England, Volume II*. London: Charles Scribner's Sons, 1908.

Benjamin, Lewis Saul. *Life and Letters of John Gay*. London: Daniel O'Connor, 1921.

Black, Jeremy. *The Hanoverians: The History of a Dynasty*. London: Hambledon and London, 2007.

Black, Jeremy. *Politics and Foreign Police in the Age of George I, 1714–1727*. London: Routledge, 2016.

Borman, Tracy. *King's Mistress, Queen's Servant: The Life and Times of Henrietta Howard*. London: Random House, 2010.

Brown, John. *Anecdotes and Characters of the House of Brunswick*. London: T and J Allman, 1821.

Campbell, Thomas. *Frederick the Great, His Court and Times. Vol II*. London: Colburn, 1844.

Campbell Orr, Clarissa. *Queenship in Europe 1660–1815: The Role of the Consort*. Cambridge: Cambridge University Press, 2004.

Christian of Schleswig Holstein. *Memoirs of Wilhelmine, Margravine of Baireuth*. New York: Scribner & Welford, 1887.

Corp, Edwin T. *Lord Burlington: The Man and His Politics*. Lewiston: Edwin Mellen Press, 1998.

Cowper, Mary. *Diary of Mary, Countess Cowper, Lady of the Bedchamber to the Princess of Wales, 1714 -1720*. London: J Murray, 1865.

Coxe, William. *Memoirs of the Life and Administration of Sir Robert Walpole, Earl of Orford, Vol I*. London: T Cadell, Jun. and W Davies, 1798.

Coxe, William. *Memoirs of the Life and Administration of Sir Robert Walpole, Earl of Orford, Vol II*. London: T Cadell, Jun and W Davies, 1798.

Croker, John Wilson (ed.). *Memoirs of the Reign of George the Second: Vol I*. Philadelphia: Lea and Blanchard, 1848.

Croker, John Wilson (ed.). *Memoirs of the Reign of George II from his Accession to the Death of Queen Caroline by John, Lord Hervey: Vol I*. London: John Murray, 1848.

Croker, John Wilson (ed.). *Memoirs of the Reign of George II from his Accession to the Death of Queen Caroline by John, Lord Hervey: Vol II*. London: John Murray, 1848.

Curties, Henry. *A Forgotten Prince of Wales*. London: Everett & Co., 1912.

Curzon, Catherine. *The Imprisoned Princess*. Barnsley: Pen & Sword Books Ltd, 2020.

Curzon, Catherine. *Kings of Georgian Britain*. Barnsley: Pen & Sword Books Ltd, 2017.

Curzon, Catherine. *Queens of Georgian Britain*. Barnsley: Pen & Sword Books Ltd, 2017.

Curzon, Catherine. *Sophia – Mother of Kings*. Barnsley: Pen & Sword Books Ltd, 2019.

Danneil, Johann Friedrich. *Das Geschlecht der von der Schulenburg: Vol II*. Salzwedel: JD Schmidt, 1847.

Daybell, James and Norrhem, Svante. *Gender and Political Culture in Early Modern Europe, 1400–1800*. London: Routledge, 2016.

Doran, John. *Lives of the Queens of England of the House of Hanover, Volume I*. New York: Redfield, 1855.

Draper, Sarah. *Memoirs of the Princess of Zell: Vol I*. London: William Lane, 1796.

Edwards, Averyl. *Frederick Louis, Prince of Wales, 1701–1751*. London: Staples Press, 1947.

Ewald, Charles Alex. *Sir Robert Walpole: A Political Biography*. London: Chapman and Hall, 1878.

Field, Ophelia. *The Kit-Cat Club: Friends Who Imagined a Nation*. London: Harper Press, 2008.

Fisher, George. *A Companion and Key to the History of England*. London: Simpkin and Marshall, 1832.

Gold, Claudia. *The King's Mistress*. London: Quercus, 2012.

Hatton, Ragnhild. *George I*. London: Thames and Hudson, 1978.

Hervey, John. *Lord Hervey's Memoirs*. London: Batsford, 1963.

Hill, George Birkbeck (ed.). *Lord Chesterfield's Worldly Wisdom*. Oxford: Clarendon Press, 1891.

Howard, Henrietta, Countess of Suffolk. *Letters to and from Henrietta, Countess of Suffolk, Vol I*. London: John Murray, 1824.

Howard, Henrietta, Countess of Suffolk. *Letters to and from Henrietta, Countess of Suffolk, Vol II*. London: John Murray, 1824.

Hunt, Margaret. *Women in Eighteenth-Century Europe*. New York: Routledge, 2010.

Jesse, John Heneage. *Memoirs from the Court of England: Vol II*. Philadelphia: Lea and Blanchard, 1843.

Kemble, John Mitchell (ed.). *State Papers and Correspondence Illustrative of the Social and Political State of Europe*. London: John W Parker and Son, 1857.

Kiste, John van der. *King George II and Queen Caroline*. Stroud: The History Press, 2013.

Laird, Mark, and Wiesberg-Roberts, Alicia. *Mrs. Delany and Her Circle*. New York: Yale Center for British Art, 2009.

Lecky, William Edward Hartpole. *A History of England in the Eighteenth Century: Vol I*. London: Longmans, Green, and Co, 1879.

Lepel [sic], Mary, Lady Hervey. *Letters of Lady Hervey*. London: John Murray, 1821.

Llanover, Lady. *The Autobiography and Correspondence of Mary Granville, Mrs. Delany: Vol I*. London: Richard Bentley, 1861.

Llanover, Lady. *The Autobiography and Correspondence of Mary Granville, Mrs. Delany: Vol II*. London: Richard Bentley, 1862.

Llanover, Lady. *The Autobiography and Correspondence of Mary Granville, Mrs. Delany: Vol III*. London: Richard Bentley, 1861.

Luttrell, Narcissus. *A Brief Historical Relation of State Affaires from September 1678 to April 1714: Vol IV*. Oxford: Oxford University Press, 1857.

Macknight, Thomas. *The Life of Henry St John, Viscount Bolingbroke*. London: Chapman and Hall, 1863.

Mahon, Lord. *History of England: Vol II*. Leipzig: Bernhard Tauchnitz, 1853.

Mahon, Lord (ed.). *The Letters of Philip Dormer Stanhope, Earl of Chesterfield: Vol II*. London: Richard Bentley, 1845.

Mangan, JJ. *The King's Favour*. New York: St Martin's Press, 1991.

Marschner, Joanna. *Queen Caroline: Cultural Politics at the Early Eighteenth Century Court*. New Haven: Yale University Press, 2014.

Martin, Peter. *Pursuing Innocent Pleasures: The Gardening World of Alexander Pope*. Hamden: Archon Books, 1984.

McGrath, Charles Ivar. *Ireland and Empire, 1692–1770*. Abingdon: Routledge, 2016.

Melville, Lewis. *The First George in Hanover and England, Vol I*. London: Sir Isaac Pitman and Sons, Ltd, 1908.

Melville, Lewis. *The First George in Hanover and England, Vol II*. London: Sir Isaac Pitman and Sons, Ltd, 1908.

Melville, Lewis. *Lady Suffolk and Her Circle*. London: Hutchinson & Co, 1924.

Melville, Lewis. *Life and Letters of John Gay*. London: Daniel O'Connor, 1921.

Melville, Lewis. *The Life and Writings of Philip, Duke of Wharton*. London: John Lane, 1913.

Melville, Lewis. *The South Sea Bubble*. London: Daniel O'Connor, 1921.

Molloy, J Fitzgerald. *Court Life Below Stairs or London Under the First Georges, Vol I*. London: Hurst and Blackett, 1882.

Pearce, Edward. *The Great Man: Sir Robert Walpole: Scoundrel, Genius and Britain's First Prime Minister*. London: Random House, 2011.

Plumb, JH. *The First Four Georges*. London: Collins, 1987.

Richardson, Jerusha. *Famous Ladies of the English Court*. Chicago: Herbert Stone & Company, 1899.

Rogers, Pat. *An Introduction to Pope*. London: Methuen & Co Ltd, 1975.

Rumbold, Valerie. *Women's Place in Pope's World*. Cambridge: Cambridge University Press, 1989.

Saussure, Cesar de. *A Foreign View of England in the Reigns of George I & George II*. London: John Murray, 1902.

Scott, Walter (ed.). *The Works of Jonathan Swift: Vol I*. Edinburgh: Archibald Constable and Co, 1814.

Scott, Walter (ed.). *The Works of Jonathan Swift: Vol VII*. Edinburgh: Archibald Constable and Co, 1814.

Sedgwick, Romney. *Some Materials Towards Memoirs of the Reign of King George II: Vol I*. London: Privately published, 1931.

Shawe-Taylor, Desmond and Burchard, Wolf. *The First Georgians: Art and Monarchy 1714–1760*. London: Royal Collection Trust, 2014.

Sinclair-Stevenson, Christopher. *Blood Royal: The Illustrious House of Hanover*. London: Faber & Faber, 2012.

Smith, Malcolm (ed.). *Human Biology and History*. London: Taylor & Francis, 2002.

Smucker, Samuel M. *A History of the Four Georges, Kings of England*. New York: D Appleton and Company, 1860.

Stanhope, Philip Dormer, Earl of Chesterfield. *Characters of Eminent Personages of His Own Time*. London: William Flexney, 1777.

Stepney to Cresset, *Dresden Despatch*, 24 July–3 August 1694.

Swift, Jonathan. *The Correspondence of Jonathan Swift: Vol II*. London: Lang, 2003.

Swift, Jonathan. *The Hibernian Patriot*. London: A Moor, 1730.

Swift, Jonathan. *Letters, Written by Jonathan Swift, DD, and Several of his Friends: Vol II*. London: T Davies, 1767.

Swift, Jonathan. *The Works of Jonathan Swift: Vol II*. London: Henry G Bohn, 1843.

Tegue, Ingrid H. *Women of Quality*. Rochester: The Boydell Press, 2002.

Thackeray, William Makepeace. *The Four Georges*. London: Smith, Elder, & Co, 1862.

Thompson, Andrew C. *George II: King and Elector*. New Haven: Yale University Press, 2011.

Toland, John. *An Account of the Courts of Prussia and Hanover*. London: John Darby, 1705.

Trench, Charles Chenevix. *George II*. London: Allen Lane, 1973.

Trowbridge, WRH. *Seven Splendid Sinners*. New York: Brentano's, 1909.

Van Muyden, Madame (ed.). *A Foreign View of England in the Reigns of George I and George II*. New York: E P Dutton and Company, 1902.

Vernon, James. *Letters Illustrative of the Reign of William III from 1696 to 1708: Vol II*. London: Henry Colburn, 1841.

Walpole, Horace. *Complete Works of Horace Walpole*. Hastings: Delphi Classics, 2015.

Walpole, Horace. *Correspondence of Horace Walpole with George Montagu Esq: Vol II*. London: Henry Colburn, 1837.

Walpole, Horace. *The Letters of Horace Walpole: Vol II*. New York: Dearborn, 1832.

Walpole, Horace. *The Letters of Horace Walpole, Earl of Orford: Vol I*. London: Lea and Blanchard, 1842.

Walpole, Horace. *Letters of Horace Walpole, Earl of Orford, to Sir Horace Mann*. London: Richard Bentley, 1833.

Walpole, Horace. *Lord Orford's Reminiscences*. London: John Sharpe, 1818.

Walpole, Horace. *Memoirs of the Reign of King George the Second: Vol I*. London: Henry Colburn, 1846.

Walpole, Horace. *The Works of Horatio Walpole, Earl of Orford: Vol IV*. London: GG and J Robinson, 1798.

Walpole, Horace and Cunningham, Peter (ed.). *The Letters of Horace Walpole, Earl of Orford: Vol I*. London: Richard Bentley, 1877.

Walpole, Horace and Wright, John. *The Letters of Horace Walpole: Vol I, 1735–1748*. Philadelphia: Lea and Blanchard, 1842.

Ward, Adolphus William. *The Electress Sophia and the Hanoverian Succession.* London: Longmans. Green and Co, 1909.

Ward, Adolphus William. *Great Britain & Hanover.* New York: Haskell House Publishers Ltd, 1971.

Ward, Sean (trans.). *Memoirs (1630–1680).* Toronto: Centre for Reformation and Renaissance Studies and ITER, 2014.

Warner, Rebecca (ed.). *Original Letters.* London: Longman, Hurst, Rees, Orme, and Brown, 1817.

Watkin, David. *The Architect King.* London: Royal Collection, 2004.

Wharncliffe, Lord. *The Letters and Works of Lady Mary Wortley Montagu*: Vol I. London: Richard Bentley, 1837.

Wilkes, Thomas (ed.). *The Works of the Reverend Dr Jonathan Swift: Vol XVI.* Dublin: George Faulkner, 1767.

Wilkins, William Henry. *Caroline, the Illustrious, Vol I.* London: J Murray, 1901.

Wilkins, William Henry. *Caroline, the Illustrious, Vol II.* London: Longmans, Green and Co, 1901.

Wilkins, William Henry. *The Love of an Uncrowned Queen.* London: Longmans, Green, and Co, 1903.

Williams, Howard. *English Letters and Letter-Writers.* London: George Bell and Sons, 1886.

Williams, Robert Folkestone. *Memoirs of Sophia Dorothea, Consort of George I, Vol I.* London: Henry Colburn, 1845.

Williams, Robert Folkestone. *Memoirs of Sophia Dorothea, Consort of George I, Vol II.* London: Henry Colburn, 1845.

Worsley, Lucy. *Courtiers: The Secret History of the Georgian Court.* London: Faber and Faber, 2011.

Wortley Montagu, Lady Mary. *The Letters and Works of Lady Mary Wortley Montagu, Vol I.* London: R Bentley, 1837.

Wortley Montagu, Lady Mary. *Letters from the Levant During the Embassy to Constantinople, 1716–18.* New York: Arno Press & The New York Times, 1971.

Wortley Montagu, Lady Mary. *The Works of the Right Honourable Lady Mary Wortley Montagu, Vol III.* London: R Bentley, 1817.

Wraxall, N William. *Memoirs of the Courts of Berlin, Dresden, Warsaw and Vienna, Vol I.* London: A Strahan, 1800.

Newspapers
All newspaper clippings are reproduced © The British Library Board; in addition to those cited, innumerable newspapers were consulted.

British Journal. 16 February 1723; issue 22.

British Journal. 5 June 1725; issue 142.

British Journal. 24 June 1727; issue 248.

British Mercury. 28 July 1714–4 August 1714; issue 474.

Daily Courant. 5 June, 1714; issue 3936.

Daily Courant. 7 August, 1714; issue 3990.

Daily Gazetteer. 24 April 1745; issue 5017.

Daily Journal. 18 May 1722; issue CCCCXII

Daily Journal. 31 May 1723; issue 735.

Daily Journal. 20 September 1727; issue 2086.

Daily Journal. 24 April 1730; issue 2901.

Daily Post. 15 June 1727; issue 2411.

Daily Post. 1 August 1728.

General London Evening Mercury. 1 November 1756; issue 549.

Grub Street Journal. 7 January 1731; issue 53.

London Evening Post. 29 May 1729–31 May 1729; issue 231.

London Evening Post. 22 June 1731–24 June 1731; issue 557.

London Evening Post. 12 July 1735–15 July 1735; issue 1194.

London Evening Post. 10 May 1743–12 May 1743; issue 2419.

London Evening Post. 28 July 1767–30 July 1767; issue 4473.

London Gazette. 29 March 1715–2 April 1715; issue 5316.

London Gazette. 29 May 1725–1 June 1725; issue 6377.

Mist's Journal. 27 May 1721.

Original Weekly Journal. 23 April 1720.

Original Weekly Journal. 28 May 1720.

Post Boy. 21 March 1700–23 March 1700; issue 773.

Post Boy. 12 January 1723–15 January 1723; issue 5224.

Post Man and the Historical Account. 3 July 1716–5 July 1716; issue 11250.

Present State of Europe or the Historical and Political Mercury. 1 May, 1692.

St James's Evening Post. 29 September 1733–2 October 1733; issue 2859.

Weekly Journal or British Gazetteer. 9 May 1719.

Weekly Journal or British Gazetteer. 30 December 1727; issue 138.

Weekly Journal or Saturday's Post. 12 August 1721; issue 141.

Wrexham Weekly Advertiser. 2 June 1888; volume 40.

Websites Consulted

British History Online (http://www.british-history.ac.uk)

British Newspapers 1600–1950 (http://gdc.gale.com/products/19th-centurybritish-library-newspapers-part-i-and-part-ii/)

Georgian Papers Online (https://gpp.royalcollection.org.uk)

Hansard (http://hansard.millbanksystems.com/index.html)

Historical Texts (http://historicaltexts.jisc.ac.uk)

House of Commons Parliamentary Papers (http://parlipapers.chadwyck.co.uk/marketing/index.jsp)

JSTOR (www.jstor.org)

The National Archives (http://www.nationalarchives.gov.uk)

Oxford Dictionary of National Biography (http://www.oxforddnb.com)

State Papers Online (http://go.galegroup.com/mss/start.do?prodId=SPOL&authCount=1)

The Times Digital Archive (http://gale.cengage.co.uk/times-digital-archive/times-digital-archive-17852006.aspx)

Index